KINSMAN REDEEMER

CODY AVERETT

FOREWORD BY OWEN BRICKELL

ISBN 979-8-35095-172-1

TABLE OF CONTENTS

Foreword

To you, cherished reader in Christ,

Before these pages came to be in book form, I had the privilege of hearing firsthand the sermons that inspired the journey you are about to embark on. As an elder at Mustard Seed Church (Mascoutah, Illinois), where these six sermons were preached the winter of 2023, I bore witness to the Holy Spirit's work in the lives of all those in attendance. In the midst of a congregation who love the word of God, there arose a newfound height and reverent awe for the Holy Scriptures. Throughout the six weeks, I witnessed tears of joy flowing from eyes uplifted by the precious pearls of God's word. Today, I witness a congregation not simply swayed by fleeting emotions, but rather forged in the purifying flames of sanctification, stirred within the crucible of our Lord's grace. I pray that these pages will bring the same encouragement to you and to those around you.

May this book not only enrich your understanding of our Lord but also serve as a constant reminder of the boundless love and grace that our Kinsman Redeemer offers. May you find comfort in His presence, assurance in His promises, and strength in His everlasting embrace. Lastly, as you journey through these words, may your faith be strengthened, your spirit uplifted, and your heart filled with the joy of salvation.

Soli Deo Gloria,

Owen Brickell

Preface

God gave many laws to Israel that, to us today, are often understood as simply strange or outdated. While helping your neighbor pull his animal out of a ditch may have been a huge problem in ancient Israel, I personally have not come across such a predicament one time in my life. Misunderstanding, or simply ignoring, these huge sections of the Bible (that is, the Mosaic and Judicial law) has caused some error in the modern church. Where it has not caused error, it has caused confusion, and in some cases, even division and legalism.

I must admit, it saddens me to see even one child of God misled or left without proper guidance in understanding the Old Testament. We ought to be able to take joy in all of God's words - yes, even Leviticus. So, when discussion came up surrounding the Old Testament topic of a kinsman redeemer, I was more than glad to lead a Bible study on it; and when asked to turn that study into a sermon series, I was all the more eager to do so.

What you have sitting in front of you right now is the result of a six-week sermon series on the type of kinsman redeemer found in Levitical law followed by the anti-type: Christ. This, of course, was not accomplished on my own; many members of my church helped in turning my manuscripts into the book you see right now. Chiefly, my Pastor took on the task of formatting and editing the entire thing, while others from the church proofread it. To everyone who has helped in making these teachings more widely available: Thank you.

This book then forms a sort of case study on how we understand judicial and ceremonial law. We do not simply ignore it, but we do handle it carefully; we cannot rid it of its historical significance, but we can see the glory of Christ shining through all of it. I pray that this book will serve as an instrument to guide readers to think deeply about the ways God has worked in the past with Israel, in order that those principles and precepts may be consistently interpreted and applied today - and this in a way that does not force legalism upon the church, yet does not ignore the glory of God's previous workings.

Church, let us not be those who are confused and flustered when asked why we wear clothing of mixed fabric and eat shrimp; but let us, through a solid understanding of the Scriptures, reply boldly that our Lord has instituted for us a new covenant that is much more glorious than anything offered in the old. Let us proclaim that God will have His people set apart, not by ceremonial law, but by the purchase of Christ. May we not be fooled by ideas that we ought to be like Israel, but let us look to our Messiah who has fulfilled all law and then died vicariously for us.

But when the fullness of time had come, God sent forth his Son, born of woman, born under the law, to redeem those who were under the law, so that we might receive adoption as sons. -
Galatians 4:4-5

Your brother in Christ,
Cody Averett

If the Son sets you free, you will be free indeed!

-John 8:36

1

Defining a Kinsman Redeemer
Leviticus 25:47-55

For quite some time, understanding the Old Testament has challenged many. Leviticus tends to be the stumbling block for most Bible reading plans. The vast of Genesis and Exodus are captivating, following stories of God working marvels for the salvation of His people. As the Bible-in-a-year plan reaches the last five Chapters of Exodus, we tend to be left scratching our heads. As you read all the intricacies of tabernacle construction it would be fantastic if you were a master architect with heaps of gold, but chances are, you are not. Then Leviticus commences, and many seem utterly lost, unsure of the text's relevance, prompting some to abandon their reading altogether.

In this first chapter, my goal is to illustrate how the Old Testament, including Leviticus, applies to you, wherever you are in life, your occupation, your home, and your relationships with fellow Christians. I aim to demonstrate that all Scripture, being God-breathed, is beneficial for teaching, rebuking, correcting, and equipping us for every good work (2 Tim 3:16-17)—even if that work resembles constructing a temple predominantly out of gold, to your surprise.

Here's the thing: there are two ways to approach this, and I'll explore both. The first is how many Christians feel when encountering texts like Leviticus—it seems irrelevant to us because it is about the law, and well, we are freed from it. Amen and hallelujah to that! The second approach involves trying to find parallels between Old Testament texts and New Testament doctrines. However, imposing New Testament ideas onto the Old Testament might lead to a skewed understanding.

For instance, if I claim Leviticus 25:47-55 speaks solely of Christ as our Redeemer, I would miss the broader context. While it is true that Christ is our Redeemer, the text had practical implications for the original audience. They would not have interpreted it solely as a reference to God as our Redeemer. Instead, they would see it as a commandment regarding what a kinsman should do if a relative sells themselves into slavery. This view of the text is also correct, but not in its entirety.

Therefore, while Christ indeed serves as our Redeemer, we should not force this interpretation onto the text to prove a point. We must grasp the text as intended by God, adhering to its natural meaning. In essence, when reading Leviticus, it means exactly what it says.

The enduring 2nd London Baptist Confession of 1689 (2LBC), held by notable theologians to include the "Prince of Preachers," Charles Spurgeon; Chapter 1 paragraph 9, asserts that "the true and full sense of any Scripture is not manifold, but one."[1] In simpler terms, each text holds a single intended meaning. It cannot signify one thing to you and something else to me. Our task is to unearth the intended message. I will not strive to make this text more compelling by drawing arbitrary connections between words and phrases. Instead, I will uncover the genuine and comprehensive essence of this Scripture and glory in the God who has given it to us.

Having established this, my aim is to convey that while this text might not directly apply to us as it did to its original recipients, we can still apply all of Scripture, including Leviticus, to our lives. In Paul's first letter to the Corinthians we are informed that the events in Israel's history were recorded for our guidance (1 Corinthians 10:11). Therefore, firstly, I will illustrate how this text does not immediately apply to you, and then I will reveal how it does. But before that, let us delve into the text itself.

---

[1] D.W. Barger, editor. The Second London Baptist Confession of Faith (Knightstown, IN: Particular Baptist Heritage Books, 2022), 13.

[47] "If a stranger or sojourner with you becomes rich, and your brother beside him becomes poor and sells himself to the stranger or sojourner with you or to a member of the stranger's clan, [48] then after he is sold he may be redeemed. One of his brothers may redeem him, [49] or his uncle or his cousin may redeem him, or a close relative from his clan may redeem him. Or if he grows rich he may redeem himself. [50] He shall calculate with his buyer from the year when he sold himself to him until the year of jubilee, and the price of his sale shall vary with the number of years. The time he was with his owner shall be rated as the time of a hired worker. [51] If there are still many years left, he shall pay proportionately for his redemption some of his sale price. [52] If there remain but a few years until the year of jubilee, he shall calculate and pay for his redemption in proportion to his years of service. [53] He shall treat him as a worker hired year by year. He shall not rule ruthlessly over him in your sight. [54] And if he is not redeemed by these means, then he and his children with him shall be released in the year of jubilee. [55] For it is to me that the people of Israel are servants. They are my servants whom I brought out of the land of Egypt: I am the LORD your God.

Why this does not apply to you:

Alfred Edersheim, a 19th-century Biblical scholar, states that the book of Leviticus instructs us on "how, having been brought near to God, the people were to maintain, enjoy, and exhibit the state of grace of which they had become partakers."[2] However, this application cannot directly extend to us as it did to God's covenant nation because we are not Israel. They were under a conditional covenant, as clearly delineated in Leviticus 26. The laws articulated in Leviticus were imperative for Israel to receive God's blessings.

Thus, says the Lord in Leviticus 26:14,

> "But if you will not listen to me and will not do all these commandments, if you spurn my statutes, and if your soul abhors my rules, so that you will not do all my commandments, but break my covenant then...(v33) I will scatter you among the nations, and I will unsheathe the sword after you, and your land shall be a desolation, and your cities shall be a waste."

Leviticus essentially outlines the regulations within the covenant between God and Israel. These were rules essential for them to obey to maintain the state of grace they were in. In fact, if we consider the entirety of Leviticus, the initial 16 chapters detail how to address sin. It is as though the first 15 chapters build up to the

---

[2] Alfred Edersheim, Bible History: Old Testament, vol. 2 (Grand Rapids, MI: William B. Eerdmans Publishing Company, 1975), 138.

pivotal day, the day of atonement, where a sacrifice cleansed the people and restored their relationship with God. Subsequently, with sin addressed and a cleansed covenant community, the latter half of Leviticus directs the Israelite community on how to live. However, the entirety of this Old Testament book pertains to a covenant that no longer exists, just as Edersheim suggests, Leviticus details "how, having been brought near to God, the people were to maintain, enjoy, and exhibit the state of grace of which they had become partakers."[3]

A fundamental aspect of this covenant was the requirement to obey the rules to receive blessings. It was the duty of the Israelites to uphold the state of grace they had entered. Jeremiah 31 reveals the brokenness of this covenant by Israel, leading to the revelation of a new covenant with God. This passage in Jeremiah 31 prompts the author of Hebrews to assert: "In speaking of a new covenant, [God] makes the first one obsolete. And what is becoming obsolete and growing old is ready to vanish away" (Hebrews 8:13).

Hebrews 8 emphasizes that **the covenant with Israel was flawed and has been replaced by a superior covenant with better promises,** allowing us to draw near to God through the precious blood of the Lamb, not through the law. The glory of this new covenant surpasses that of the old; it eliminates the distance between God and humanity, offering Israel a superior hope. As Jesus told the woman at the well, there is no longer a temple where God's covenant

---

[3] Edersheim, 138.

people must worship—everyone who draws near to God through Christ can worship in Spirit and truth! (John 4:24).

Leviticus, with its sacrificial rituals and regulations, no longer applies to anyone. For "the blood of bulls and goats can never take away sins" (Hebrews 10:4). Considering Leviticus 25:2, where the Lord commands Moses to speak to the people of Israel about observing the Sabbath when entering the land given by God, sheds light on the context of v47-55. **God addresses the people of Israel in a specific land, circumstances that do not align with our present reality.** We are not a physical community of Israelites, nor do we reside in land allotted by God to each tribe of Israel.

To further clarify why this text does not apply to us: **The concept of a kinsman redeemer is rooted in a tribal commitment.** This is most evident in Numbers 36, where women inheriting land must marry within their tribe to retain the land within it. Similarly, a kinsman redeemer reinstates land or a destitute brother into his original tribe. In Leviticus 25:35-46, a kinsman redeemer is not required if a person sells himself to his brother, only if to a stranger or foreigner.

Therefore, since we lack tribes with specific land portions designated by God, this text cannot apply to us as it did to Israel. Leviticus 25:47-55 concludes by declaring the reason for kinsman redeemers: Israelites are God's servants whom He brought out of the land of Egypt. We were not enslaved in Egypt and were not delivered from its bondage.

Wrap-up:
I hope I have sufficiently clarified that this text does not directly apply to you in the same manner it did to the Israelites it was initially directed to. This passage no longer holds relevance for anyone in that specific context because that covenant no longer exists; the surpassing glory of the cross has far exceeded the glory of the law. God states in Jeremiah 31 that Israel is no longer under any conditional covenant. Instead, God has promised to redeem Israel with the assurance that "they will all know me, from the greatest to the least. I will forgive their iniquity, and I will remember their sin no more" (Jeremiah 31:34).

Now, an evident question arises: How can we affirm that all Scripture is beneficial for teaching while simultaneously claiming that this particular text does not apply to us at all? This question leads me to my second objective, which is to illustrate how this text does indeed have relevance for you. However, to achieve that, we must first grasp the essence of the text.

Why this does apply to you:

In Verse 8 of Chapter 25, we encounter the jubilee. **This year was a time of immense rejoicing for the people of Israel—a year symbolizing liberty and restoration.** It commenced on the tenth day of the seventh month, coinciding with the day of atonement. On this significant day, the high priest put on his linen garments with bells and entered God's presence with the blood of a bull, making atonement for himself and

8

his family. Subsequently, he would enter again with the blood of a lamb, purifying the most holy place from Israel's defilement. Any misstep by the priest in God's presence could result in death. Perhaps there was a sense of relief as the high priest exited the holy of holies, having completed his task successfully. Amidst these pivotal events, a great trumpet blast resounded, heralding liberty throughout the land—a poignant reminder to the Israelites: "Rejoice! You're no longer enslaved to Egypt—rejoice, brethren, for your God has freed you from those chains!"

This heralded the beginning of the jubilee year—a time when labor ceased, and God Himself provided for His people from the fields. For that year, it might have felt, in some small sense, like a return to the pre-cursed Garden of Eden. There was no toil or struggle for sustenance; God provided abundantly without the sweat of their brow. Furthermore, at the sound of the trumpet, any sold land reverted to its original owner. Those who had sold themselves into slavery were now free. Liberty resonated throughout the land.

All the toil and labor of the previous six years ceased during this year. If you were enslaved, now you were free! Had you sold your land? The jubilee joyously declared it was once again yours. The Lord would provide produce in the fields; there was no need for labor! At the sound of the trumpet, a full year of freedom and rest commenced.

The jubilee marked the focal point of all sales. Whenever land was sold, it was never a perpetual sale. The value of land was calculated based on the number of harvests until the jubilee year. Verse 23 emphasizes this, stating, "The land shall not be sold in perpetuity, for the land is mine. For you are strangers and sojourners with me." Even the covenant nation of Israel, inheriting the land promised by God, did not have complete authority over it; they were mere strangers on it—the land belonged to God. Hebrews 11 underscores that those entering Canaan still saw themselves as strangers and exiles, yearning for a greater inheritance (Hebrews 11:13-16). The promised land for Israel was merely a shadow; God had prepared a city for His people!

This truth held tremendous glory. **Within this covenant, no one had the right to oppress another.** Your brother could not dominate you. The land belonged to God, and He determined its fate, assigning each tribe its designated land. Pursuing this idea to Verse 25, we begin to discern the role of a kinsman redeemer. "If your brother becomes poor and sells part of his property, then his nearest redeemer shall come and redeem what his brother has sold."

A kinsman redeemer's role within Israel was to restore what had been lost. The Dictionary of Bible Themes defines a kinsman redeemer as *the relative who restores or preserves the full community rights of disadvantaged family members.* This aligns with the jubilee—a provision by God for Israelites to attain freedom before its arrival. A destitute man, who had reached the brink and sold his means of sustenance for himself and his family—his field—could be redeemed by a brother. The repurchase of his field echoed the jubilee's liberty bell ringing prematurely. His lost position within the covenant community had been reclaimed by his brother—an entire restoration of his community rights facilitated by his kinsman's grace. God's provisions for His people did not end there. Consider Verse 35. "If your brother becomes poor and cannot maintain himself with you, you shall support him as though he were a stranger and a sojourner, and he shall live with you." Throughout this chapter, God commands care for His people. This care does not manifest through miraculous intervention but through men who fear God and willingly obey. When an Israelite loses his land, God does not magically create new property for him from the heavens, although He could if He chose to. Instead, God employs those who submit to His commands and ordinances—men whom He delivered from slavery into possession of their land. **It is through ordinary means that God benefits His people.**

Interestingly, Leviticus 25 labels all of Israel as strangers and foreign residents in the land owned by God. Now, if a brother becomes poor—a situation all of Israel once faced—they are to support him as they would a stranger or foreign resident. How does God support you? That is how you should support your brother. Did He provide you land when you had none? Food in your time of need? Did He lavish you with blessings? Your God rescued you from Egypt and sustains you; you should reciprocate the same to your kinsman.

11

In ancient Israel, if your brother loses his land, the responsibility falls on you to redeem it. The same care for your brother would prompt you to support him if he cannot sustain himself. If I am your Israelite brother and you fall into poverty, I should not exploit you for my own gain. We were both once impoverished and enslaved in Egypt, toiling without reaping the fruits of our labor. Now, God has united us as brothers in this vast land, and you have fallen into poverty once more. Should not I use whatever means God has granted me from His land to support you?

The passage further explains that even if your brother descends into such dire straits as to sell himself to you, it is imperative not to treat him as a slave but employ him as a worker. Under this covenant, we exist not solely for our individual welfare but for the community's benefit. **You are your brother's keeper, his redeemer, even.**

God's commands differ for those outside the covenant nation. They can be your slaves, but your brother cannot. Why? Look to Leviticus 25:38, where God proclaims, "I am the LORD your God, who brought you out of the land of Egypt to give you the land of Canaan, and to be your God." This aligns with the reasoning in Verse 17, "You shall not wrong one another, but you shall fear your God, for I am the LORD your God." It is as if the LORD is saying, "I am Yahweh, your covenant God, the great I Am who can do all things. I rescued you from the oppressor; cannot you do the same for your brother? I liberated you from the oppressor; how dare you ever consider oppressing

12

your brother? That brother is my slave, whom I bought for myself. He cannot belong to both of us, so you must treat him like a brother." How could the Israelites position themselves to rule over one another ruthlessly when led by the God who so patiently extends grace? They were all to serve One Master.

There is one more scenario outlined in Leviticus 25, which provides one of the Bible's best definitions of a kinsman redeemer. Verse 47 states, "If a stranger or sojourner with you becomes rich, and your brother beside him becomes poor and sells himself to the stranger or sojourner with you or to a member of the stranger's clan, then after he is sold, he may be redeemed. One of his brothers may redeem him, or his uncle or his cousin may redeem him, or a close relative from his clan may redeem him. Or if he grows rich he may redeem himself."

If your land is sold to someone else, it can be redeemed, or you regain it in the jubilee year. You cannot be enslaved to a fellow Israelite, and even if you become their hired worker, you are set free in the jubilee year. But what if a stranger purchase you? What if you end up in another clan? If that is your sole means of survival, you have become so desperate to sustain yourself that you are willing to forsake your heritage. God provides a way back—without waiting for the jubilee year. Your brother, uncle, cousin, or a close relative has the right, given by God, to bring you back to the clan. You have divine protection on your side; the covenant your nation abides by stipulates that you can be redeemed. Your owner must comply with these terms. "And" as God emphasizes in Verse 54, "if he is not redeemed by these means, then he and his children with him shall be released in the year of jubilee. For it is to me that the people of Israel are servants. They are my servants whom I brought out of the land of Egypt: I am the LORD your God."

Once more, we are informed of the rationale behind these commands. **The reason behind the Jubilee and kinsman redeemers is that Israel belongs to God**. They are His possession, so they must be free from all others. God has pledged them this land, and now we see that He has established means to restore Jews who lose their portion of the promise. It is the Israelites' obligation to their close relatives to restore them whenever they stumble, to take on the role of a kinsman redeemer, and to restore and safeguard the full community rights of disadvantaged family members.

How does all of this fit into where we are right now? How can we take a passage so specific to a certain people, at a particular time, under a covenant that no longer exists, and apply it to our current situation? We live in a time where land ownership can be indefinite (as long as taxes are paid), where slavery is not legal, and where the population is diverse, not all adhering to a single covenant.

The answer lies in a doctrine known as "general equity." According to Merriam-Webster, equity *is a body of legal doctrines and rules developed to enlarge, supplement, or override a narrow rigid system of law.* In Leviticus, we encounter a narrow and inflexible legal system, yet beneath that lies a general moral principle in the text. The strict system dictates how the law applies in specific circumstances, but the moral duty behind it extends to people of all ages. So, even though we will not find ourselves in a situation where a brother's status and livelihood depend on us buying back his sold land, we can comprehend from the text that God desires us to care for our brothers.

The 2LBC, in Chapter 19, states that God "gave various judicial laws"[4] to Israel, where judicial implies that these laws were punishable if disobeyed. These laws expired with the state of that people and no longer bind anyone due to that institution; their general equity, however, remains morally applicable.

Question: What is the clear moral message proclaimed in Leviticus 25? Answer: Care for God's covenant people.

Be Reminded of the words of the Apostle Paul:

> "Brothers, if anyone is caught in any transgression, you who are spiritual should restore him in a spirit of gentleness. Keep watch on yourself, lest you too be tempted. Bear one another's burdens, and so fulfill the law of Christ. For if anyone thinks he is something, when he is nothing, he deceives himself. But let each one test his own work, and then his reason to boast will be in himself alone

---

[4] D.W. Barger, editor. The Second London Baptist Confession of Faith (Knightstown, IN: Particular Baptist Heritage Books, 2022), 139.

and not in his neighbor. For each will have to bear his own load. Let the one who is taught the word share all good things with the one who teaches. Do not be deceived: God is not mocked, for whatever one sows, that will he also reap. For the one who sows to his own flesh will from the flesh reap corruption, but the one who sows to the Spirit will from the Spirit reap eternal life. And let us not grow weary of doing good, for in due season we will reap, if we do not give up. So then, as we have opportunity, let us do good to everyone, and especially to those who are of the household of faith." (Galatians 6:1-10)

The exact same moral message is proclaimed to us today, to be applied within our covenant community - the household of faith. God morally binds each and every one of us to bear one another's burdens. We are commanded by God in 1 Corinthians 10:24 not to seek our own good, but the good of our neighbor. The last two sentences of James say, "My brothers, if anyone among you wanders from the truth and someone brings him back, let him know that whoever brings back a sinner from his wandering will save his soul from death and will cover a multitude of sins" (James 5:19-20).

You have the opportunity to be a kinsman redeemer. We have the duty from God to watch over our brethren, to know when they are struggling - whether that be physically or spiritually. May God help us be attentive to each other's needs, to be a community of believers that watches out for one another and protects one another. By the grace of God, we can be a people that put others before ourselves. Do you see your brother caught in transgression? Pull him out. Remember, it was not a supernatural interworking that God used to restore land to someone who lost it; it was a close brother who saw the need and met it.

Conclusion:

In Leviticus 25, we witness an involved community, a people who looked out for one another and treated each other as family. You do not need some special revelation that descends from the clouds to tell you your purpose in the church. In Leviticus 25:47-55, God clearly employs the average Israelite to accomplish the most glorious ends. The church exists for you, and as a community, we are given to each other by God for each other. Take pains to see the opportunities God gives you to care for your brother.

Let me restate the definition of a kinsman redeemer one more time: Your job within the church is to be *the relative who restores or preserves the full community rights of disadvantaged family members.* Where is your brother or sister not receiving what is rightfully theirs from Christ's church? Be the one who ensures those blessings are given. Where is your brother or sister disadvantaged? Be the redeemer who, in likeness to your Savior, bears their burden and gives them the advantage. How fallen and far off were you when your precious Savior called you to Himself and gave you every spiritual blessing in the heavenly places? How deep in the trenches of slavery to sin were you? Did you have any right to the covenant of grace when Christ gave you a place in the kingdom? Oh, dear Christian, beloved reader, you did not deserve any of the redemption Christ gave you - so give freely to your people without seeking return.

One more piece of application:
A kinsman redeemer also preserves the community rights of his fellow citizens. We must not only react when our brothers and sisters fall; we must hold them up so that they do not fall. Exhort one another daily so that no one will fall into the pains of sin. Be proactive in encouraging one another in the abundant riches of Christ so that we may all be encouraged and not even consider finding joy elsewhere. Warn of the dangers of sin, so that no one would dare to toy with such evil against our great God.

And why must we act like this? **Because we are God's possession.** We must not allow our brothers and sisters to fall to anyone.
In the words of the 19th-century hymn writer George Askins:

Let us love our God supremely,
Let us love each other too
Let us love and pray for sinners,
Till our GOD makes all things new

Then He'll call us home to heaven,

18

at His table we'll sit down
Christ will gird Himself and serve us
with sweet manna all around

Leviticus is not a dead and lifeless book to be ignored. The covenant may change, the people may change, the application may change, but does our God ever change? Most assuredly not. Jesus Christ is the same yesterday, today, and forever. The way in which we love our neighbor will vary based on the situation, but the command remains the same. Leviticus provides us with abundant examples of how reflecting God's moral character is expressed in different circumstances. We have been given the great privilege to read it and see the immense love God has for His covenant people.

Moreover, Leviticus 25 shadows One who will bring in a greater Jubilee and be the chief Kinsman Redeemer:

> "The Spirit of the Lord is upon me, because he has anointed me to proclaim good news to the poor. He has sent me to proclaim liberty to the captives and recovering of sight to the blind, to set at liberty those who are oppressed, to proclaim the year of the Lord's favor." (Luke 4:18-19)

Jesus Christ came proclaiming the year of God's favor—the great Jubilee. Are you in bondage to sin? Christ blows the trumpet of freedom. Are you poor, wretched, and pitiful? Christ proclaims good news to you. Are you oppressed by the tyranny of that great serpent, the devil? Christ has come to set you at liberty. Are you blind? Christ can give eyes to see.

Our great Savior, worth more than all the riches of the world combined and multiplied infinitely, descended to earth to purchase our redemption with His blood. As we will explore in the coming chapters, He takes on the role of our Kinsman Redeemer as He restores us to the community rights we had before the fall. Our redeemer purchases us, not with perishable things like silver or gold, but with His own blood. Remember, the year of jubilee did not begin until the day of atonement. It was when that sacrificial offering was made that liberty was proclaimed. Rejoice, Christian, for your freedom has been purchased at the cross. Moreover, your freedom from death has been provided by your Christ, who rose from the dead and now sits in heaven to intercede for you and preserve your full community rights as a child of God and a citizen of Heaven.

2

Ruth's Redemption
Ruth 4:13-22

Let the sobering words from our Lord to Israel resound deep into your soul:

"I brought you up from Egypt and brought you into the land that I swore to give to your fathers. I said 'I will never break my covenant with you, and you shall make no covenant with the inhabitants of this land; you shall break down their altars.' But you have not obeyed my voice. What is this you have done? So now I say, I will not drive them out before you, but they shall become thorns in your sides, and their gods shall be a snare to you' (Judges 2:1-3).

Judges goes on to describe the state of the nation:

> "The people of Israel did what was evil in the sight
> of the LORD and served the Baals. And they
> abandoned the LORD, the God of their fathers,
> who had brought them out of the land of Egypt.
> They went after other gods, from among the gods
> of the peoples that were around them, and bowed
> down to them. And they provoked the LORD to
> anger...The anger of the LORD was kindled
> against Israel, and He gave them over to plunderers
> who plundered them. And He sold them into the
> hand of their surrounding enemies, so that they
> could no longer withstand their enemies. Whenever
> they marched out, the hand of the LORD was
> against them for harm, as the LORD had warned,
> and as the LORD had sworn to them. And they
> were in terrible distress" (Judges 2:11-15).

In the annals of history, the state of Israel had plunged
into moral decay so profound that the Lord Himself
depicted them as a nation straying from their
faithfulness, consumed by pursuits of false affections.
Despite God's enduring patience, the inevitable
consequences foretold in His covenant now unfolded—
the weight of curses upon this unfaithful bride.

Imagine if you were amidst Israel during these
turbulent times, peace would have eluded you. Your
nation's actions had transgressed God's standards,
leading to their surrender into the clutches of the
Midianites. Their oppressive rule forced countless of

23

your kin to seek refuge in the desolate mountains, hiding within caverns and dens. Fields once tended with care were now ravaged; pastures devoid of oxen and donkeys, all slaughtered by the enemy. Hope crumbled as adversaries multiplied like an uncountable swarm of locusts. The once-mighty army that brandished the banner of the Lord now fell prey to the relentless might of your foes. The desperate pleas to lifeless idols echoed unheard while the true God seemed to have withdrawn His favor. Yet, in the face of these adversities, indifference flourished, and disdain for God's commandments ran deep. Thus, Israel found itself at its lowest ebb.

The righteous anger of God kindled against them, meting out judgment that placed them beneath the dominion of their adversaries. Instead of victory, they encountered repeated defeat. If you were living in Israel during this era, hopelessness would have cloaked you; who could rescue you from such a relentless onslaught?

This brings me to the pivotal text I wish to explore in this chapter—Ruth 4:13-22. Picture yourself dwelling in Israel during the reign of the Judges, perhaps inhabiting the unassuming town of Bethlehem. Once a lush landscape ripe for farming, now reduced to barren dust under the looming judgment of God. The land suffered from a scarcity of grain, inadequate even to sustain livestock or families. The promised land, once brimming with abundance akin to milk and honey, now bore neither.

Amidst this bleakness were your acquaintances, Elimelech and Naomi, accompanied by their two sons,

Ephrathites hailing from Bethlehem. They grappled with the severity of the famine, prompting Elimelech's decision to relocate his family to Moab, a foreign, pagan land, forsaking their covenant ties to Israel.

A decade elapsed without their return, yet contrary to Elimelech's beliefs, the Lord had not abandoned His people. God intervened, providing sustenance that rekindled hope as people reveled once more in bountiful provisions, a gift from the Lord. Life appeared to inch back to normalcy. Then, a ripple of excitement coursed through the town—a widow named Naomi emerged after a decade-long absence. A widow? What transpired during her absence?

"Do not call me Naomi," she declared, "call me bitter, for the Almighty has dealt harshly with me." It was apparent that the Lord's hand weighed heavily upon her; widowed, devoid of both sons, with only Ruth, a Moabite, by her side. Over time, it became known that Ruth was the widow of one of Naomi's sons.

In the midst of this era marked by anguish and upheaval, amid Israel's veering towards false gods and facing divine retribution, one truth remained unwavering: God reigned supreme. Amidst the unending unrest and agony within the humble enclave of Bethlehem, history was poised to unfold.
As the 19th-century hymn writer Phillips Brooks so eloquently penned:

> *"O little town of Bethlehem,*
> *How still we see thee lie,*

25

Above thy deep and dreamless sleep,
The silent stars go by;
Yet in thy dark street shinest Thee everlasting light;
The hopes and fears of all the years Are met in thee
tonight. "

Rejoice and marvel in the glorious word of the Living
God; Chapter 4 of Ruth, beginning in Verse 13.

"So, Boaz took Ruth, and she became his wife.
And he went in to her, and the Lord gave her
conception, and she bore a son. Then the women
said to Naomi, "Blessed be the Lord, who has not
left you this day without a redeemer, and may his
name be renowned in Israel! He shall be to you a
restorer of life and a nourisher of your old age, for
your daughter-in-law who loves you, who is more
to you than seven sons, has given birth to him."
Then Naomi took the child and laid him on her lap
and became his nurse. And the women of the
neighborhood gave him a name, saying, "A son has
been born to Naomi." They named him Obed. He
was the father of Jesse, the father of David.

Now these are the generations of Perez: Perez
fathered Hezron, Hezron fathered Ram, Ram
fathered Amminadab, Amminadab fathered
Nahshon, Nahshon fathered Salmon, Salmon
fathered Boaz, Boaz fathered Obed, Obed fathered
Jesse, and Jesse fathered David" (Ruth 4:13-22).

This passage marks the final verses in the captivating narrative of Ruth, unwrapping the sequence of events. Yet, Boaz's kindness toward Ruth did not sprout suddenly. Our initial glimpse of him appears in Chapter 2, where the writer paints him as a commendable man hailing from Naomi's late husband's lineage. This swift introduction of Boaz acts as a precursor to what unfolds next. Shortly after, in the succeeding verse of Chapter 2, Ruth ponders seeking favor in someone's field to glean from. It is almost as if Verse 1 serves as a tantalizing hint, stirring predictions based on the unveiled details. We encounter this "worthy man," Boaz, identified as a "relative of Naomi," alongside Ruth's quest for a benefactor for her gleaning endeavors. The anticipation of who that figure might be lingers in the air.

God had already decreed provisions for field gleaners in His law, stating, "When you reap the harvest of your land, you shall not reap your field right up to its edge, neither shall you gather the gleanings after your harvest. And you shall not strip your vineyard bare, neither shall you gather the fallen grapes of your vineyard. You shall leave them for the poor and for the sojourner: I am the LORD your God" (Leviticus 19:9-10). This law was intended to provide sustenance for foreigners in dire need. Ruth appeared well-versed in this practice and seized the opportunity. During times post-famine, many would have greedily hoarded their harvests. Boaz, however, took a different path, guided by the principle found in "Whoever despises his neighbor is a sinner, but blessed is he who is generous to the poor" (Proverbs 14:21).

Boaz not only grants Ruth permission to glean but extends further, shielding and providing sustenance while she toils. What propels Boaz? He sacrifices his own provisions to assist a foreigner. She is not even an Israelite; she herself admits her unworthiness to be called his servant, yet he treats her as his own. He permits her to glean amidst the harvesters and instructs them to leave bundles for her.

In Boaz, we witness more than mere compliance with the law's literal demands; he embodies its underlying principles and general equity. He does not perceive the law as a burdensome set of rules but as a blueprint for nurturing a compassionate, empathetic community. Boaz willingly supports this young foreigner, acknowledging her worthiness and community-oriented spirit. He ardently loves the Lord, acknowledges his own forebears as foreigners, and regards all his possessions as gifts from God's benevolent hand. Consequently, he extends love to his neighbor and aids the impoverished foreigner.

Amidst the act of gleaning, Boaz's words to Ruth resonate deeply: "The LORD repay you for what you have done, and a full reward be given you by the LORD, the God of Israel, under whose wings you have come to take refuge!" How starkly it contrasts Naomi's bitterness with Boaz's exuberance in the Lord!? Naomi, embittered after leaving God's covenant land, stands in stark contrast to Boaz's unwavering joy in God and His law, affirming the Lord as Ruth's sanctuary.

28

Yet, the narrative's tension remains unresolved. While God continues to provide for Ruth and shelter her under His wing, the means by which this occurs are diminishing. The harvest season, serving as Ruth's link to Boaz draws to a close. The provider and protector, Boaz, is moving on, leaving Ruth and her mother-in-law once more facing an uncertain future. While the Lord remains Ruth's ultimate refuge, she is losing the immediate protection symbolized by Boaz's sheltering wing.

Ruth takes a significant step in Chapter 3, asking Boaz to spread his wings over her and be her redeemer. In the last chapter, we defined a kinsman redeemer as *someone who restores or preserves the full community rights of disadvantaged family members.* Here, we witness Boaz embodying that role, not just by adhering to the strict letter of the law. What we see is not a man hesitant to comply with the LORD's commands but someone who gladly embraces his duty to God and His people, regardless of the personal cost. Boaz's response embodies a commitment: "As the LORD lives, I will see to it that you are redeemed."

To echo a profound truth, allow me to quote Carl Delitzsch:

> "According to the theocratical rights, Jehovah was the actual owner of the land which He had given to His people for an inheritance; and the Israelites themselves had merely the [right to enjoy the use] of the land which they received by lot for their

inheritance so that the existing possessor could not part with the family portion or sell it at his will, but it was to remain forever in his family. When anyone therefore was obliged to sell his inheritance on account of poverty, and actually did sell it, it was the duty of the nearest relation to redeem it as goël (goël – Hebrew for redeemer)."

Moreover, Deuteronomy 25 stipulates that if a man's married brother dies, it becomes the living brother's duty to take the widowed woman as his own and father a child with her, ensuring the continuity of his deceased brother's name.

While Boaz was not Ruth's brother-in-law, he was a close relative. This emphasizes his kindness towards her, revealing that his actions stemmed from genuine affection for his family and, most importantly, for the LORD of his family. The law of Levirate marriage, mandating a brother to marry his sister-in-law, might not directly apply to Boaz if taken solely by its literal interpretation. Nevertheless, Boaz rejoices in understanding the spirit behind the law and in loving as his LORD loves.

In what universe does Ruth deserve any of this? She herself declared unworthiness, unfit even to be considered a servant, let alone the wife of Boaz. If she were an Israelite, there might be some covenant value, but she is a Moabite. Deuteronomy 23 sternly states, "No Ammonite or Moabite may enter the assembly of the LORD... You shall not seek their peace or their prosperity all your days forever." Everything about

Ruth contradicts her, suggesting that this should not work. What kind of God takes the destitute and the wretched, and molds something beautiful out of such misery? It does seem confounding, does it not? What sort of godly man is this who gazes upon Ruth, a woman seemingly offering nothing in return, only entreating him to provide her with what he possesses? In what world does this narrative, where someone humbly pleads for what they lack, make any logical sense?

Yet, when we glimpse into a world orchestrated by a sovereign and compassionate God, this narrative unfolds as part of a grander design. It is a realm where God's grace defies conventional wisdom. This godly man, Boaz, operates not on the principles of mere reciprocity but on the tenets of a higher purpose, driven by compassion and kindness rather than transactional gains. In this divine economy, generosity and selflessness supersede expected returns.

In a world guided by a sovereign and gracious God who acts as He pleases for the good of His people, it all makes perfect sense. Boaz acquires the land that belonged to Elimelech. And with that land comes Ruth the Moabite. Let me restate that: **Ruth the Moabite. The outcast, the pagan, the enemy, from a place abhorred by God. With the land comes Ruth the Moabite.**

Therefore, Ruth 4:13 is awe-inspiring to read: "So Boaz took Ruth." This is not a scripted love story. The magnificence here is not in the romantic tale falling into place; it is the unfolding of God's redemption plan. We get to read Ruth and witness how God utilizes man, someone who brings nothing to the table and creates abundance out of void.

This narrative also glimpses the other side—an ordinary man fervently devoted to his God. He does not do anything extraordinary or complex; he simply obeys his LORD. I observe an average servant of God being employed in a purpose so immense that it surpasses my understanding.

Remember how this whole narrative began? It was God's retribution upon an unrighteous people. A family left the covenant nation, thinking they might discover more blessing in a pagan land, yet it all turned to despair. But upon their return to Bethlehem, God's blessings began to rain down.

Ruth, the woman possibly married for a decade in Moab without a child? In a fleeting moment, we read Verse 13: "Boaz took Ruth, she became his wife. He went in to her, the LORD gave her conception, she bore a son."

But the blessings are not limited. Our attention shifts from judgment, famine, and widowhood to this divine blessing upon Ruth, Naomi, and the child. In Verse 14, Naomi is blessed and receives a redeemer. Yet, it does not end there; the child himself is blessed with renown in Israel. This child, Obed, becomes the father of Jesse, who is the father of David—of whom it is inscribed in 2 Samuel 5:13 that the LORD established him as king over Israel and exalted his kingdom for his people's sake.

The essence of a kinsman redeemer commenced in Egypt with Pharaoh's enslaved people, but it culminates here with God's servants entering His land to serve and abide by His laws. Our story in Ruth began with God's condemnation upon disobedience, yet it culminates with the lineage of one obedient man, Boaz, from whom King David is descended. It is this David who brings the ark of the LORD to Jerusalem, dancing fervently before God. 2 Samuel 7 illuminates how through this great King, the LORD granted Israel rest from all their surrounding adversaries.

Conclusion:

Ruth's journey began in utter turmoil, yet the redeemer, an ordinary man acting out of love for his kin, takes Ruth as his wife. This act of blessing extends not only to Ruth or Naomi but ripples through the entire nation of Israel. But the blessings do not halt there. In 2 Samuel 7:12, God promises King David, "I will raise up your offspring after you, who shall come from your body, and I will establish his kingdom." And in Verse 16, "Your house and your kingdom shall be made sure before me. Your throne shall be established forever."

Reflect on Verse 18 of Ruth Chapter 4: "Now these are the generations of Perez: Perez fathered Hezron, Hezron fathered Ram, Ram fathered Amminadab, Amminadab fathered Nahshon, Nahshon fathered Salmon, Salmon fathered Boaz, Boaz fathered Obed, Obed fathered Jesse, and Jesse fathered David" (Ruth 4:18-22). From David's line came Jeconiah, the great-grandfather of Zerubbabel, whose lineage included Eleazer. Eleazer fathered Matthan, who fathered Jacob, the father of Joseph, the husband of Mary, through whom Jesus, called Christ, was born.

Why is this concept of the kinsman redeemer so pivotal? It became the means through which God brought forth Christ—our ultimate redeemer. A narrative that commenced with a judge concludes with a King. What began in obscurity culminates in illumination. A childless widow becomes the mother of a child who brings peace to the nations whose dominion stretches from sea to sea.

No more exile for God's people; our great King has arrived. He surpasses even the greatness of David, demonstrating unwavering faithfulness to His people. Our majestic King laid down His life to grant us citizenship in His kingdom. David was an extraordinary king, yet he perished, his body succumbing to decay. Our mighty God did not abandon Christ to the grave; our Savior arose through the power of the Spirit. Elevated to the right hand of our Father in the heavens, reigning until every adversary is brought under His rule.

Fear not, Israel! Fear not, children of God! You have a magnificent King who crushes your adversaries. Every foe will be trampled underfoot, like the mire of the streets. Remain steadfast during times of famine. Be faithful when it appears the enemy is prevailing. Fear not even in distress, amid turmoil, with adversaries encircling you. You are part of a kingdom that shatters every other dominion.

At the beginning of Ruth, Israel may have seemed widowed of hope. Yet, God provided a kinsman redeemer, through whom He brought forth a superior redeemer. Thus, our tale concludes where it began:

"O little town of Bethlehem,
How still we see thee lie,
Above thy deep and dreamless sleep,
The silent stars go by;
Yet in thy dark street shinest Thee everlasting light;
The hopes and fears of all the years Are met in thee
tonight."

3

Christ Our Kinsman
Psalm 22:1-24

Psalm 22 is a composition by David filled with sorrow and suffering, yet it concludes with glory. While the exact time of its composition in David's life is uncertain, it is evident that he grappled with profound struggles. This is metaphorically depicted through animals devouring him, intense physical pain, and self-depreciation.

David, not merely an ordinary man in Israel, held the position of king. Thus, this Psalm raises questions about the apparent disorder and injustice. Why is a king portrayed in such a lowly state, and more importantly, why is there no one to assist him? Towards the end of the Psalm, we discover that this King, pushed to the brink of death, is singing praises to his God among his brethren.

Johannnes H. Ebrard reflects on this by stating:

> "If now the first, the imperfect David, considered it
> an essential part of his Messianic calling to love his
> subjects as brethren in God, to care for the
> salvation of their souls, and to elevate them to his
> own relation of sonship to God—how could the
> second, the perfect David, be inferior to him in
> this?[5]"

In Hebrews 2:12, the author quotes Verse 22 of Psalm 22 to illustrate that Christ is not ashamed to call us brothers. Despite the struggles depicted in the Psalm, when the Lord exalts Him back to His throne, Christ doesn't trample on His subjects but rejoices with them as brothers. The goal is to present Christ as a brother— a figure who suffered, experienced pain, and faced rejection, yet sympathizes with our weaknesses without sinning.

Consider the definition of a Kinsman Redeemer: "a relative who restores or preserves the full community rights of a disadvantaged family member." Christ fulfills this role for us—a brother who knows and understands us, made the perfect Redeemer through shared suffering. Our Redeemer is flesh and blood—He is human.

---

[5] Ebrard, Hebrews, 349. Quoted by Martin. Exegetical and Theological Commentary on the Epistle to the Hebrews. Trinity Pulpit Press, Montville, New Jersey, 2020. 121

John Owen emphasizes:

> "This is a ground of unspeakable consolation unto believers, with supportment in every condition. No unworthiness in them, no misery upon them, shall ever hinder the Lord Christ from owning them, and openly avowing them to be His brethren. He is a brother born for the day of trouble, a Redeemer for the friendless and fatherless. Let their miseries be what they will, he will be ashamed of none but of them who are ashamed of him and his ways.[6]"

And Calvin, speaking of Christ's humanity says:

> "What, then, of man: plunged by his mortal ruin into death and hell, defiled with so many spots, befouled with his own corruption, and overwhelmed with every curse? In undertaking to describe the Mediator, Paul then, with good reason, distinctly reminds us that He is man: "One mediator between God and men, the man Jesus Christ" [1 Tim. 2:5]. He could have said "God"; or he could at least have omitted the word "man" just as he did the word "God." But because the Spirit speaking through his mouth knew our weakness, at the right moment he used a most appropriate

---

[6] John Owen, An Exposition of the Epistle to the Hebrews, ed. W. H. Goold, vol. 20, Works of John Owen (Edinburgh: Johnstone and Hunter, 1854), 423.

remedy to meet it: he set the Son of God familiarly among us as one of ourselves."[7]

As we delve into Psalm 22, you'll observe its striking familiarity. While David wrote it concerning his own suffering, it prophetically proclaims the greater King seated on David's throne—Christ. In this Psalm, Christ is not merely mentioned; He is the one speaking. David serves only as a type and shadow of the coming Christ, who will undergo the depicted agony on a much grander scale. Keeping this perspective in mind, let's proceed to read the perfect, inerrant, word of the living God.

Psalm 22:1-24

[1] My God, my God, why have you forsaken me?
    Why are you so far from saving me, from the
        words of my groaning?
[2] O my God, I cry by day, but you do not answer,
        and by night, but I find no rest.
[3] Yet you are holy,
        enthroned on the praises of Israel.
[4] In you our fathers trusted;
        they trusted, and you delivered them.
[5] To you they cried and were rescued;
        in you they trusted and were not put to shame.

[7] John Calvin, Institutes of the Christian Religion & 2, ed. John T. McNeill, trans. Ford Lewis Battles, vol. 1, The Library of Christian Classics (Louisville, KY: Westminster John Knox Press, 2011), 465.

6 But I am a worm and not a man,
   scorned by mankind and despised by the people.

7 All who see me mock me;
   they make mouths at me; they wag their heads;

8 "He trusts in the LORD; let him deliver him;
   let him rescue him, for he delights in him!"

9 Yet you are he who took me from the womb;
   you made me trust you at my mother's breasts.

10 On you was I cast from my birth,
   and from my mother's womb you have been my
   God.

11 Be not far from me,
   for trouble is near,
   and there is none to help.

12 Many bulls encompass me;
   strong bulls of Bashan surround me;

13 they open wide their mouths at me,
   like a ravening and roaring lion.

14 I am poured out like water,
   and all my bones are out of joint;
   my heart is like wax;
   it is melted within my breast;

15 my strength is dried up like a potsherd,
   and my tongue sticks to my jaws;
   you lay me in the dust of death.

16 For dogs encompass me;
   a company of evildoers encircles me;
   they have pierced my hands and feet—

17 I can count all my bones—
   they stare and gloat over me;

18 they divide my garments among them,

and for my clothing they cast lots.
19 But you, O LORD, do not be far off!
     O you my help, come quickly to my aid!
20 Deliver my soul from the sword,
     my precious life from the power of the dog!
21 Save me from the mouth of the lion!
     You have rescued me from the horns of the wild
          oxen!
22 I will tell of your name to my brothers;
     in the midst of the congregation I will praise you:
23 You who fear the LORD, praise him!
     All you offspring of Jacob, glorify him,
     and stand in awe of him, all you offspring of
          Israel!
24 For he has not despised or abhorred
     the affliction of the afflicted,
and he has not hidden his face from him,
     but has heard, when he cried to him.

With a resounding cry, the entire Psalm begins with the well-known phrase, "My God, My God, why have you forsaken me?" David, too, experienced a profound sense of being forsaken by God, yet in his faith, he clung to the hope that the Lord remained his God. His proclamation wasn't a cry to a distant God unrelated to him, but to a close God who seemed to have forsaken him.

There are times when we may also feel this way, especially when our faith is weak and the light provided by our God seems dim. In those moments of darkness, we find ourselves crying out, trying to understand what is happening. Like David in this Psalm, we may cry day and night and struggle to find rest. Yet, despite the challenges, we hold on with everything we have to that precious title, "my God," knowing that ultimately, our faith will emerge victorious.

For Christ, this heightened experience reached its peak. In the days of Christ's flesh, it is recounted that He offered loud cries and tears to the One able to save Him from death. In the garden of Gethsemane, He was so sorrowful and troubled that the agony felt like it could lead to death. Such was the intensity of His suffering that our Elder Brother sweated drops of blood.

This profound pain and agony accompanied Him to the cross, where He exclaimed, "My God, My God, why have You forsaken me?"

John Andrewes explains:

"God indeed had forsaken him until his anger was pacified, and his wrath appeased. Notwithstanding that he feeleth himself as it were wounded with God's wrath, and forsaken for our sins, yet he ceaseth not to put his confidence in God, and call upon him…it was our sins, and the heavy burden thereof…which this deeply tormented Christ did undergo. Through the which our sins, & iniquities, God was so highly displeased, that they being laid upon his son's shoulders, made him to cry out with a loud voice, about the ninth hour of the day, saying, O my God, my God, why hast thou forsaken me?" [8]

Christ found no rest in His pleading with God; He stayed up all night in that garden, awaiting His death. Yet, despite the apparent despair, faith prevailed. **Despite the challenging circumstances outlined in Verses 3-5, David emphasizes that God remains the Deliverer.** David's circumstances do not alter the holiness of God, and God continues to be the Deliverer of his fathers. Throughout history, God has consistently redeemed His people, requiring only their patient waiting. Though the struggle may be difficult, those who trust in God have never been put to shame.

Christ, too, proclaims God as the Deliverer of His fathers (His human ancestry). Importantly, if we understand this Psalm as prophetic of Christ, we see Him crying out to God, similar to David. In Christ, we do not have a Redeemer incapable of sympathizing with our weaknesses. Christ associates Himself as a descendant of the fathers of Israel. We witness Christ in a state of distress and weakness, placing Himself alongside those who call out to God for rescue and help. The inner struggle involves recognizing the holiness of God while grappling with the apparent lack of answers and the turned face of God. "But You are

---

[8] Andrewes, John. The Golden Cabinet of True Treasure. London: John Crosley, 1615. Early English Books Online Text Creation Partnership, 2011.

the God of my Fathers, and you answered them when they called to You for help! But me..."

In Verses 6-8, Christ reveals Himself in a lowly state, declaring, "I'm not helped - I'm being regarded as a worm and not a man." As Calvin puts it, this portrays one who is "abased beneath all men, and, as it were, cut off from the number of living beings."[9] It raises the question: Could it be that the Son of God, the great and glorious Christ, full of beauty and splendor, is despised by mankind to the extent that He appears as a worm, lacking any form or appearance that would attract their attention?

In this depiction, there is a mockery of the infinitely Holy One. The Son of God is subjected to disdain by humanity, with no semblance of beauty that would draw their gaze. The mockery inflicted upon our greater David runs deep and is painful. They sneer at His relationship with God, insinuating that He is entirely estranged from the deliverer and rescuer of Israel. In the minds of these mockers, there seems to be no possibility that this man would be rescued from his inevitable death.

In Verses 9-11, Christ expresses trust in the Father to deliver Him. He reflects on the Lord sustaining Him from birth until now, with the assurance that past experiences indicate continued sustenance as long as God wills it. Christ acknowledges that it was God who instilled trust in Him, making it unthinkable

---

[9] John Calvin and James Anderson, *Commentary on the Book of Psalms*, vol. 1 (Bellingham, WA: Logos Bible Software, 2010), 366.

for God to forsake Him. In times of abandonment by friends and unity among enemies, Christ turns to God for help, pleading for His presence when others have turned away.

It is crucial to note that Christ entrusts Himself to His faithful Father, the God who has sustained Him throughout His life. Even in the face of numerous enemies and bearing the reproaches directed at God, Christ remains resolute. He becomes a stranger and alien to His brothers, and even the drunkards make songs about Him. Despite the profound struggles, Christ continues to place His trust in God. Moreover, it's essential to recognize that Christ's earthly life was marked by a deep struggle depicted vividly as shedding blood. The intensity of His struggle is portrayed to the extent that blood is shed—a level of struggle that surpasses any we may have faced. Our Christ, dear brothers and sisters, felt every bit of the pain in this profound struggle, as evident in Verses 12-18.

In Verses 12-18, David vividly describes the pain he is experiencing—surrounded by enemies, fear making his mouth dry, heart feeling like melting wax, and hands and feet pierced. He is entrapped, pleading with God to deliver him from the hand of his enemies. Christ undergoes a similar ordeal, surrounded by great bulls in the form of those from the forest of Bashan, seeking to devour Him like lions tearing apart prey.

Jesus is poured out like water, stretched out on the tree, His heart melting as life drains from Him. He struggles as strength leaves Him, mouth dry, tongue sticking to the roof, and the Father lays Him in the dust of death. There is a threefold pain: **first**, the anguish of mankind rebelling against Him, the loneliness of having no one on earth to seek help, and the shame of being stripped of His clothes, with people casting lots for them. **Secondly**, Christ endures physical pain—poured out like water, bones out of joint, strength gone, and hands and feet pierced. His unimaginable pain is a testament to the depth of His understanding when we experience physical suffering. **Thirdly**, Christ faces the agony of being forsaken by God. As Verse 15 indicates, it was God who laid Him in the dust of death. God gave His life to those who were His murderers, evildoers, dogs, and bulls. With enemies numerous and God seemingly laying Him in the dust of death, Christ calls out for help. The pain He endures encompasses physical agony, the rejection of mankind, and the apparent forsaking by God.

In Verses 19-21, Christ calls out for help in the midst of immense pain and agony as death tightens its grip. The cords of death encompass and tighten so strongly that there seems to be no plausible escape. It is a depiction of standing before the greatest enemy and succumbing to its grip.

Christ's life is fading away, and the only deliverer now is God. In times of need, God alone is our strength and a very present help. The soul Christ speaks of, the life that must be delivered from the power of the dog, is His only soul and life. Christ pleads with the Father to rescue Him from the mouth of the lion. In Verse 21, we read, "You have rescued me from the horns of the wild oxen."

In Verse 21, Christ receives help, and it's noteworthy that throughout this Psalm, the enemies of the King are depicted as animals maliciously attacking their prey. They are dogs encompassing, strong bulls of Bashan surrounding, a roaring lion, and here, an ox with the great force of his horns ready to fight. Despite these formidable adversaries, Christ is delivered from death.

Our Christ, who died as a man, was raised as a man. He was our brother then, and He remains our brother now. In the grave for three days, He was raised to life by the power of God, never to face death again. It befits our Redeemer that if He suffered as a man, He is also glorified as a man. Thus, we read of His great praise as the Lord delivers Him from the formidable enemy—death.

In Verses 22-24 Christ glorifies God. His response is highly significant, revealing the reality of His condescension. Amidst all His suffering, mocking, flogging, being forsaken, and afflicted, He remained our brother. Now, in glory and eternally raised from the dead, Christ declares in Verse 22, "I will tell of Your name to my brothers." Our great Savior calls us His own, proclaiming God's name to us as we become part of His family.

When David spoke of brotherhood, it was limited to the physical descendants of Abraham. David's brotherhood was confined to blood relations. However, Christ, as our Kinsman, is not bound by blood. Just as Ruth was closely related to Boaz by covenant rather than blood, so it is with us and our Redeemer.

47

Archibald M'Lean emphasizes that "Christ, by professing his faith or trust in God, declares Himself to be a son of Abraham, consequently related as a brother to all who believe, whether Jews or Gentiles, they having the same Spirit of faith.[10]"

While our King is exalted to the infinite pinnacle of glorification, He remains near to His people. We are part of Christ's congregation, praising the Father with Him. This doctrine is wonderful because, regardless of where you are in life, you have a High Priest who can sympathize with you. Christ is not ashamed to call you His brother.

John Brown beautifully illustrates the significance of Christ's brotherhood:

"Suppose two friends, equally benevolent in their temper, equally attached to you: the one, a person who had never suffered under the afflictions to which you are exposed; the other, one who had experienced the same, or at least a very similar course of trials. Would there not be a tenderness, and a suitableness, and a minuteness of appropriate attentions and consolations experienced from the latter, which, in the very nature of things, it is

---

[10] M'Lean, Hebrews, 119. Quoted by Martin. Exegetical and Theological Commentary on the Epistle to the Hebrews. Trinity Pulpit Press, Montville, New Jersey, 2020. 124

impossible that the former, however kindly disposed, should yield?[11]"

Conclusion:

Do you feel as though God has forsaken you? Take heart; if you are a believer, Christ has been forsaken so you do not have to be. When we, like David here, cry out wondering why God has forsaken us, we can be reminded of our Brother who was pierced for our transgressions and crushed for our iniquities. This isn't to drive ourselves into a mournful state, thinking that our crying and pleading is unwarranted. On the contrary, we are reminded that our Savior understands. He has been cast off and afflicted in a much greater way, so He can sympathize with us where we are right now. Are you lowly and afflicted? Your Elder Brother was brought so low that He took the name of a worm. Those closest to you may scorn and despise you, but you have a friend that will never leave your side. Let the mocking come our way; our enemies can wag their heads at us - for there is a coming day when our Lord will deliver us and exact vengeance on His adversaries. We who delight in our Lord will be brought to glory!

Our Christ had to trust our God from birth; our kinsman has gone before you and has trusted His God through and through. From the toddler years, pre-teen, teen, to young adulthood - Christ was there, fighting

---

[11] Brown, Hebrews, 137. Quoted by Martin. Exegetical and Theological Commentary on the Epistle to the Hebrews. Trinity Pulpit Press, Montville, New Jersey, 2020. 136

against the sins of those ages. Not only did He fight, but our King was victorious! When God seemed far from Him, had forsaken Him, and He realized there was none to help, no person in all of creation who could assist Him, He was hated by those whom He had created - yet Christ continued calling out to His Father.

His enemies were strong, like the bulls of Bashan, surrounding Him and opening their mouths wide to devour Him. There is no amount of pain and torture that you can endure here that Christ cannot sympathize with you. Christ went through all of that pain forsaken by God, but He has promised that He will be with you unto the ends of the earth!

So, whether it's disaster or grief, pain and sorrow, your life may be poured out like water, all of your bones out of joint. The pain can be so burdensome that your heart melts within your breast, and with no strength remaining, you lay in the dust of death. Dogs encompassing and evildoers encircling, staring and gloating, stealing what little bit you have left. Your Christ is not far off; His death has delivered you from death, and His resurrection from the power of the dog. The mouth of the Lion has no power over you, believer, for you are Christ's and Christ is God's, and that God-man Jesus Christ has brought you nearer to the throne than any saint under the old covenant was ever able to get.

So, praise Him, you who fear the LORD, glorify Him, you offspring of Jacob. Stand in awe, all of you offspring of Israel! Our God has never despised or abhorred His saints. We may be afflicted in every way, but we are not crushed; perplexed but not driven to despair, persecuted but not forsaken, struck down but not destroyed - always carrying in the body the death of Christ so that the life of Jesus may be manifested in our mortal flesh. Christ is so near to you, flesh of your flesh and bone of your bone; He has the same Father you have, spiritually and physically.

Father Abraham had many sons - I am one of them, and so are you, so let's all praise the LORD. I end this chapter with a simple plea: "Come, ye sinners, poor and needy, weak and wounded, sick and sore. Jesus stands ready to save you, full of pity, love, and power. Come, ye weary, heavy-laden, lost and ruined by the fall; if you tarry till you're better, you will never come at all." Our Jesus invites you to come and find rest in Him; He proclaims that His yoke is easy and His burden is light. The burden you carry right now, that eternal weight of sin, can only be cast off by a Savior who has defeated sin forever. Make no mistake, I have portrayed a compassionate Christ in this chapter, but I by no means believe in a weak Christ. Our Brother, who is so understanding of our weaknesses, sits as the eternal King in the heavens and will judge all sinners with eyes like a flame of fire.

4

Our Land Redeemed
Hebrews 3:7-4:11

In our exploration of kinsman redeemers, we learn that a kinsman redeemer intervenes to reclaim the land of a disadvantaged family member. Having established that Christ serves as our Kinsman, this chapter I aim to illustrate how Christ redeems the land that was lost during the fall. In the eloquent words of John Milton, the day we witnessed "paradise lost" is now transitioning into the day when "paradise regained" becomes a reality. The magnificent land that our Lord graciously placed under our authority was stripped away the day Adam sinned. However, in the exhortation ahead, we witness the grace of Christ, who pays the sin-debt and restores us to that cherished land.

7 Therefore, as the Holy Spirit says,
   "Today, if you hear his voice,
8 do not harden your hearts as in the rebellion,
      on the day of testing in the wilderness,
9 where your fathers put me to the test
      and saw my works for forty years.
10 Therefore I was provoked with that generation,
   and said, 'They always go astray in their heart;
      they have not known my ways.'
11 As I swore in my wrath,
      'They shall not enter my rest.' "
12 Take care, brothers, lest there be in any of you an evil, unbelieving heart, leading you to fall away from the living God. 13 But exhort one another every day, as long as it is called "today," that none of you may be hardened by the deceitfulness of sin. 14 For we have come to share in Christ, if indeed we hold our original confidence firm to the end. 15 As it is said,
   "Today, if you hear his voice,
   do not harden your hearts as in the rebellion."
16 For who were those who heard and yet rebelled? Was it not all those who left Egypt led by Moses? 17 And with whom was he provoked for forty years? Was it not with those who sinned, whose bodies fell in the wilderness? 18 And to whom did he swear that they would not enter his rest, but to those who were disobedient? 19 So we see that they were unable to enter because of unbelief.

4 Therefore, while the promise of entering his rest still stands, let us fear lest any of you should seem to have failed to reach it. ² For good news came to us just as to them, but the message they heard did not benefit them, because they were not united by faith with those who listened. ³ For we who have believed enter that rest, as he has said,

"As I swore in my wrath,
'They shall not enter my rest,' "

although his works were finished from the foundation of the world. ⁴ For he has somewhere spoken of the seventh day in this way: "And God rested on the seventh day from all his works." ⁵ And again in this passage he said,

"They shall not enter my rest."

⁶ Since therefore it remains for some to enter it, and those who formerly received the good news failed to enter because of disobedience, ⁷ again he appoints a certain day, "Today," saying through David so long afterward, in the words already quoted,

"Today, if you hear his voice,
do not harden your hearts."

⁸ For if Joshua had given them rest, God would not have spoken of another day later on. ⁹ So then, there remains a Sabbath rest for the people of God, ¹⁰ for whoever has entered God's rest has also rested from his works as God did from his.

¹¹ Let us therefore strive to enter that rest, so that no one may fall by the same sort of disobedience. (Hebrews 3:7-4:11)

There is a rest and it has yet to be inherited
This section of the epistle serves as a warning to the recipients, highlighting the peril of disobedience to God. The line of reasoning is clear: God established a rest at the world's foundation; however, your forefathers, due to disobedience, were unable to enter that rest. Today, the promise of rest endures, and it is crucial to trust in God to inherit it. The unfolding statements in this exhortation can be observed as follows:

In Verse 11 of Chapter 3, God declares, "as I swore in My wrath, they [the first generation of Israelites in the wilderness] shall not enter my rest." Subsequently, in Verse 18, a rhetorical question arises, asking, "to whom did [God] swear that they would not enter His rest but to those who were disobedient." The author then conclusively states in Verse 19 that "they were unable to enter because of unbelief." This progression of thought serves as a tender reminder of the consequences of disobedience and the importance of faith in inheriting the enduring rest promised by God, thus setting the stage for an exhortation in Chapter 4:1. The author acknowledges that those in the past could have entered God's rest but failed due to disobedience, Verse 1 urges, "therefore, while the promise of entering His rest still stands, let us fear lest any of you should seem to have failed to reach it." The reminder from Psalm 95 in Verses 3 and 5 emphasizes God's oath to that generation of Israelites, stating, "they shall not enter my rest." However, Verse 6 provides hope, affirming that "it remains for some to enter it," despite the failure of those who initially received the good news.

To dispel the notion that only that generation missed the rest, the author brings up Joshua. Appointed by God to lead the next generation into Canaan, Joshua successfully fulfilled his role. While one might assume that the promise has found its fulfillment through Joshua. In Verse 8, the Holy Spirit swiftly dismisses such thoughts, stating, "if Joshua had given them rest, God would not have spoken of another day later on." This underscores that the promised rest extends beyond Joshua's time, reinforcing the enduring nature of the promise.

To provide clarity on the author's statement, it's important to note that Psalm 95, attributed to David, was composed many years after the Israelites had successfully conquered the promised land. However, within the Psalm, a warning is issued against hardening hearts to prevent entering the rest of God. The persistence of God speaking about entering His rest long after the promised land's conquest implies that this rest is still available.

Furthermore, Psalm 95 was directed to people already living in the promised land who were yet to enter God's rest. This raises a crucial question: What is this rest? The ongoing mention of entering the rest, even in a time when the promised land had been attained, suggests that the "rest" of God goes beyond physical territories and earthly conquests. It prompts us to delve deeper into understanding the spiritual significance and nature of this rest that God offers.

What is this rest?

First and foremost, it's crucial to recognize that the
promised land and the land of rest are synonymous.
Let's revisit Chapter 3, Verse 7. This verse quotes
Psalm 95, which, as mentioned earlier, discusses
Israel's disobedience preventing them from inheriting
the promised land. Verse 8 highlights two key words:
"disobedience" and "testing." These words replace the
literal places mentioned in Psalm 95:8, namely Meribah
and Massah. In Hebrew, these two words convey the
equivalent of disobedience and testing, and the author
utilizes them in this passage. This choice may be due to
the audience's familiarity with the terms, emphasizing
the broader message of the passage – one that, as I aim
to demonstrate, is more about future glory than physical
boundaries.

I express all of this to arrive at my main point: the
references to Meribah and Massah and God "swearing
in His wrath" allude to Numbers 14:21-23. In this
passage, our Lord declares,

"But truly, as I live, and as all the earth shall be
filled with the glory of the LORD, none of the men
who have seen my glory and my signs that I did in
Egypt and in the wilderness, and yet have put me to
the test these ten times and have not obeyed my
voice, shall see the land that I swore to give to their
fathers. And none of those who despised me shall
see it." and again in the same chapter, God tells

57

Moses "Say to them, 'As I live, declares the LORD, what you have said in my hearing I will do to you: your dead bodies shall fall in this wilderness, and of all your number, listed in the census from twenty years old and upward, who have grumbled against me, not one shall come into the land where I swore that I would make you dwell, except Caleb the son of Jephunneh and Joshua the son of Nun."

Hence, it becomes evident that when Hebrews mentions this "rest," it is, at least partially, alluding to the land of Canaan, which the first generation of Israelites never inhabited. Described in Ezekiel 20:6 as "the most glorious of all lands," Canaan was a land flowing with milk and honey. However, the complexity deepens, as we have established that even Joshua, who inherited the land of Canaan, did not provide the Israelites with true rest.

To comprehend this concept, we must delve into the original promise. The significance of the land of Canaan lies in God's promise to Abraham in Genesis 17:8, assuring him and his offspring of its inheritance as an everlasting possession. Yet, two apparent issues arise 1. Abraham did not inherit the land before his death, and 2. None of us can have an everlasting inheritance because we all experience mortality.

This leads us to another crucial question: how do we inherit the rest that Hebrews speaks of? At this point, it's pertinent to mention that for our Kinsman Redeemer to secure our land as an everlasting possession, the ability to overcome death is imperative. However, before delving further into that aspect, let's gain a better understanding of this promised rest.

It's now clear that we are, at least in part, referring to a physical piece of land with specific boundaries promised by God to Abraham. This land, described as glorious and abundant, could rightfully be considered a place of rest. The author of Hebrews provides additional specificity in Hebrews 4:4, stating that this rest is not merely Canaan. According to Hebrews, it is something God created since the foundation of the earth. Therefore, it appears that Canaan was only a shadow of a greater rest available for entry.

In Hebrews 4:4, the author emphasizes that God's works were finished from the foundation of the world. Despite swearing in His wrath that those people wouldn't inherit the rest, it still remains available for us today. The rest remains unchanged, even though the people were disobedient.

To illustrate this concept differently, consider the creation narrative: God worked for six days and rested on the seventh. This seventh-day rest, as indicated here, is an eternal rest accessible to God's people. Therefore, after humanity's fall into sin, leading to the forfeiture of the land of rest they were in, God works throughout history to restore man to this rest.

In a covenant with Israel, God promises rest in Canaan contingent upon their obedience. However, due to their disobedience, they never experience this rest. Nonetheless, this doesn't alter the fact that God still has a rest reserved for His people. Our Lord remains steadfast in His promise to Abraham. If the promise to Abraham was not clear enough, the connection to the seventh day of creation solidifies the eternal nature of this rest. Those inheriting God's rest will be there forever. This eternal quality is emphasized in Verse 9, stating that "there remains a Sabbath-keeping for the people of God."

The term translated as "sabbath rest" in the ESV is *sabbatismos* (σαββατισμὸς), which literally means "sabbath-keeping." Notably, the word "remains" is a present verb, indicating that this sabbath-keeping is currently available. What adds complexity to this sentence is that the word *sabbatismos* is exclusively used in this passage. In the New Testament, the common term for the sabbath is derived from the root *sabbaton* (σάββατον), which simply means sabbath or the sabbath day. The word *sabbatismos* might have been coined by the author of Hebrews, suggesting that he created this term to convey the current state where a sabbath rest remains.

- DBL Greek defines the word as "a sabbath observance"[12]
- Pocket Lexicon says "a resting as on the sabbath"[13]

---

[12] James Swanson, Dictionary of Biblical Languages with Semantic Domains: Greek (New Testament) (Oak Harbor: Logos Research Systems, Inc., 1997).
[13] Alexander Souter, A Pocket Lexicon to the Greek New Testament (Oxford: Clarendon Press, 1917), 229.

- Concise dictionary gets even more specific and says "the repose of Christianity (as a type of heaven)"[14]

John Owen links this word to the Hebrew term used to express God's rest in Genesis 2. Consequently, he concludes that the word, "being so of old... is used by our apostle to show that the rest which he now asserts for the people of God is founded in the rest of God himself. If this had not been the case, it might have been *anapausis* (ἀνάπαυσις), "a rest" in general; it could not have been *sabbatismos*, "a sabbatism," a "sabbatizing rest," for there is no foundation for any such name or thing but in the rest of God."[15]

To clarify, the Greek word typically translated as "rest" in this chapter is *katapausis* (κατάπαυσίν) or something similar, until we reach this verse. Here, the author makes a deliberate switch in vocabulary to assert emphatically that a specific kind of rest remains—one related to God's rest in creation. It's important to note that the Sabbath rest of the Israelites was rooted in the same concept—a anticipation of the rest that God created at the foundation of the world. Our *sabbatismos* (σαββατιομός) here does not refer to God's covenant with Israel, which is concluded. Instead, it speaks of the rest of God Himself, a rest that we earnestly desire!

---

[14] James Strong, A Concise Dictionary of the Words in the Greek Testament and The Hebrew Bible (Bellingham, WA: Logos Bible Software, 2009), 64.

[15] John Owen, An Exposition of the Epistle to the Hebrews, ed. W. H. Goold, vol. 21, Works of John Owen (Edinburgh: Johnstone and Hunter, 1854), 325.

It logically follows that Verse 10 informs us that when we enter the final rest, we will experience a cessation of our works, mirroring God's rest at creation. This is a comprehensive rest, unparalleled and yet to be inherited by anyone. It encompasses rest from sin, labor, striving, pain, tears, and sorrow. It signifies a grand Jubilee, where the flesh is liberated from corruption, the sinner from sin, and the debtor from debts. In this era, the lame will leap, the deaf will hear, and the dead will live again. It is a time when Christians will joyfully sing that all toiling is utterly finished. Our sole purpose will be to relish the eternal presence of our God.

To recap the apostle's argument: God has established a rest from the foundation of the world; the Israelites were invited to enter this rest but failed, leaving it for us to enter. Those of faith currently experience some form of Sabbath as we eagerly await the time when we will rest from our labors, akin to God's rest. This rest, if compared to God's, must be unimaginably glorious!

This promised land that we seek is the same as Abraham who we are told lived in tents as a foreigner because he was "looking forward to the city that has foundations, whose designer and builder is God." Abraham was never looking for rest on this side of eternity: the land of Canaan could not have provided that: he was looking beyond that to the unseen. He was looking for a kingdom that cannot be shaken. In the words of Dr. Robert Paul Martin, *"the writer implies that because [God is the architect and builder of our*

62

city] our inheritance is infinitely more substantial and secure than any structure framed by us as our earthly home."[16]

And as Matthew Henry says:

> "it is a city, a regular society, well established, well defended, and well supplied: it is a city that hath foundations, even the immutable purposes and almighty power of God, the infinite merits and mediation of the Lord Jesus Christ, the promises of an everlasting covenant, its own purity, and the perfection of its inhabitants: and it is a city whose builder and maker is God. He contrived the model; he accordingly made it, and he has laid open a new and living way into it, and prepared it for his people; he puts them into possession of it, prefers them in it, and is himself the substance and felicity of it"[17]

Hebrews 12:22 continues to reveal that we "have come to Mount Zion and to the city of the living God, the heavenly Jerusalem, and to innumerable angels in festal gathering, and to the assembly of the firstborn who are enrolled in heaven, and to God, the judge of all, and to the spirits of the righteous made perfect, and to Jesus, the mediator of a new covenant, and to the sprinkled

---

[16] Robert Martin, Exegetical & Theological Commentary on the Epistle to the Hebrews (Trinity Pulpit Press, 2020), 579.

[17] Matthew Henry, Matthew Henry's Commentary on the Whole Bible: Complete and Unabridged in One Volume (Peabody: Hendrickson, 1994), 2399.

blood that speaks a better word than the blood of Abel."
Moreover, in Verse 28 of the same chapter, it declares
that we have received "a kingdom that cannot be
shaken."

How and when does someone inherit this rest?

The explicit teaching of this passage underscores that
entry into this rest is achieved through faith. In
Hebrews 3:19, we learn that the wilderness generation
failed to enter due to unbelief. Furthermore, in Verse 2
of Chapter 4, it is emphasized that the good news they
heard did not benefit them because of their lack of
belief. We partake in God's promise by believing it, as
indicated in Verse 3, which states, "we who have
believed enter that rest." However, it's crucial to note
that this doesn't mean we enter the rest immediately;
rather, those who have believed the promise will enter
the rest at the appointed time.

Verse 11 urges us to strive to enter God's rest - a
profound concept where we put forth effort now and
experience rest later. During our time on earth, we
engage in toil in accordance with God's promise, fully
aware that a time is approaching when striving will be
unnecessary. This striving to enter God's rest clarifies
that it is not something we currently possess; instead, it
is an inheritance to be received after we exert effort.
The rest and striving are presented as opposing
experiences.

The central theme of this chapter of Hebrews
revolves around the Israelites striving to reach the

promised land but ultimately failing to enter due to unbelief. This wasn't a one-time event with the initial profession of faith; rather, it required constant striving and perseverance to enter the rest. In 3:14, it is emphasized that those who share in Christ are the ones who hold their original confidence firm to the end. The examples provided in Verses 16-19 illustrate individuals who initially appeared redeemed from slavery but failed to persist in that redemption, thereby missing out on inheriting the promise. The promise is reserved for those who maintain unwavering belief, and belief is depicted as a continuous and enduring commitment.

Verse 6 of Chapter 4 underscores that those who previously received the good news failed to enter due to disobedience. The book of Hebrews conveys that belief in the promise necessitates corresponding actions. In simpler terms, if you genuinely believe that you will inherit the promised land, your actions will naturally align with that belief. To illustrate, if someone promised you a beautiful house next week, one that surpasses your current residence, and you believe that promise, would you start packing and preparing to move?

This constant exhortation in the chapter emphasizes the need to ensure that "today" one's heart is not hardened to enter the promised land. Chapter 3 provides the exhortation to encourage one another, preventing the hardening caused by sin, as a hardening from sin stems from faithlessness. Those who lack faithfulness to the promise do not receive it. It is, therefore, crucial for the church to care for one another, ensuring that everyone lives in accordance with the understanding that this world is not our permanent home. As strangers and foreigners, we aim to inherit a better city with foundations. The transient nature of worldly possessions contrasts with the enduring promise of God. The gospel promise stands forever, unlike the passing things of this world.

However, Verse 10 poses a question. If we have yet to inherit this rest, as indicated throughout the passage, what does Verse 10 mean? The ESV suggests that "whoever has entered God's rest has also rested from his works as God did from his." The Legacy Standard Bible (LSB) provides a more literal translation, stating, "For the one who has entered His rest has himself also rested from his works, as God did from His."[18] Notice the crucial distinction here. We are not necessarily talking about a general "whoever" but rather a singular past-tense action where somebody entered into God's rest. Let me propose that this somebody is Christ. Recall Verse 9, which mentions that a sabbath rest remains for God's people. Verse 10 provides the explanation for Verse 9, using the Greek conjunction *gar*, translated as "for" in both the ESV and the LSB, indicating that we are about to learn the reasoning behind Verse 9. We can interpret Verses 9 and 10 in this way: "There remains a sabbath-keeping for the people of God, because Christ who entered His rest also rested from His works as God did from His."

---

[18] *Legacy Standard Bible* (Three Sixteen Publishing, 2022), Heb 4:10.

If this verse were referring to us entering into rest, it wouldn't be termed "our rest." We enter into God's rest, but Christ, being God, can enter into His own rest after completing the work on the cross. This distinction is of utmost importance. If you've been drifting during this discussion, I urge you to pay attention to this part.

Jesus states in John 5:36 that the Father gave Him works to accomplish, and He is actively fulfilling them. Throughout Christ's entire life, He obediently followed the Father in every aspect. Then, as He went to the cross, after completing everything the Father had tasked Him to do, He declared, "It is finished!" When God placed Adam in the garden, He commanded him not to eat from a certain tree, warning that "the day you eat of it, you will surely DIE." The cost of redeeming us to enter the land is death. When Christ proclaimed "it is finished," He yielded His spirit and died. He bore the price we should have paid, taking the death we should have experienced and enduring the wrath that should have fallen on us. The subsequent aspect, however, provides hope for the promise because to enter the rest, one must be alive. Therefore, Christ, resurrected from the dead by the glory of the Father, entered as our forerunner into His rest.

The entire creation groans, experiencing the pains of childbirth as it awaits its redemption. Although it has not happened yet, continue striving, Christian, because a day is approaching when this world will be restored by fire. The promised Canaan will be ours for eternity, a land flowing with milk and honey where toil and striving will be no more.

In that future realm, there will be no more death or mourning. Every believer will enter this great rest, following behind Christ, and will cease from their works as God did from His. Emphasizing this point: Christ will redeem this land, just as He will redeem your body. We won't exist as ethereal souls floating in the clouds like bumper cars. The rest inherited by those in Christ is physical and genuine. It is the true promised land, an eternal inheritance for God's people that will never be lost. In this redeemed world, we will have hands, feet, buildings, and food – the world will be restored by our Kinsman Redeemer!

We have a brother, one who shares our flesh, and he has gone ahead of us into our rest. One day, he will redeem this land we currently inhabit, along with these mortal bodies we dwell in. This will enable us to spend eternity glorifying the Father, Son, and Holy Spirit, experiencing an eternal redemption by an eternal Redeemer!

Conclusion:

The first point arises directly from Hebrews 4:11: "Let us therefore strive to enter that rest so that no one may fall." This is a collective striving among believers. We should dedicate our lives to the pursuit of this promise. "For to this end, we toil and strive because we have our hope set on the living God, who is the Savior of all people, especially of those who believe." - 1 Timothy 4:10. If you believe in the glorious nature of the rest as described in the Bible, then strive to enter it! Hebrews

4:1 advises us to fear lest anyone fail to enter. There are those who hold fast to their confidence, boasting in their hope, and there are those who shrink back and face destruction. Believe in God's promise, for we are not among those who shrink back and are destroyed, but among those who have faith for the preservation of our souls. If you are united by faith with the Giver of this precious promise, then toil and strive with your hope set on the living God.

As this world and our bodies are destined for redemption, engage wholeheartedly in whatever your hand finds to do, for the place you are headed is filled with wisdom, knowledge, work, and thought (Ecclesiastes 9:10). I believe this aligns with Paul's message at the end of 1 Corinthians 15, where he concludes that remarkable chapter by urging, "Therefore, my beloved brothers, be steadfast, immovable, always abounding in the work of the Lord, knowing that in the Lord your labor is not in vain." Paul dedicates the entire chapter to detailing the resurrection of the dead, emphasizing that the bodies we will have in eternity are the same bodies resurrected—transformed and heavenly, yet still bodies. According to Paul, as these mortal bodies put on immortality, the works we engage in for the Lord now will not be in vain.

The entire book of Ecclesiastes explores the labor of man under the sun, deeming it all as vanity due to mortality. However, after Christ's resurrection, the perspective shifts, and our toil is no longer in vain because we have the hope of eternal life. The preacher in Ecclesiastes questions, "What does man gain from all the toil at which he toils under the sun?" To this, Paul responds, "The Lord will glorify your toil that you do in Him." The resurrection of Christ brings purpose and significance to our labor, transforming it from vanity to an endeavor that will be glorified by the Lord.

5

Christ Frees the Slave
John 8:31-36

Four chapters ago, we saw in Leviticus 25 that a Kinsman Redeemer has the duty of redeeming a poor brother from slavery. Not only that, we defined a Kinsman Redeemer as 'a relative who restores or preserves the full community rights of a disadvantaged family member.' In Chapter 2, we saw how Christ came from a lineage that was preserved by the Kinsman Redeemer Boaz. After that, we read about Christ being our Kinsman by His partaking of our flesh and blood, bringing us to the previous chapter where we spoke of Christ being a Kinsman Redeemer by redeeming a poor brother's land. We, of course, are the poor brothers. In this chapter, having established already that Christ is

72

our Kinsman, we look here at John 8 to see how Christ redeems the slave.

In Leviticus 25, we read that if a brother in the Israelite community were to become so poor and hopeless that he sells himself into the hands of a foreigner, then after he is sold, he may be redeemed. One of his brothers may redeem him, or his uncle, cousin, close relative, or even he can redeem himself. This, of course, seems great, but eventually, God's covenant people ran into a much bigger problem - the entire nation went into slavery in Babylon for their disobedience to their LORD.

In order for a brother to redeem another, at least one of the brothers has to be free. If the entire nation is in bondage, then you need a greater Redeemer than someone who is merely richer than you. The Jewish nation spent around seventy years in slavery to Babylon, and then, as documented by Ezra and Nehemiah, some of them returned to their homeland under the prophetic ministry of Zechariah and Haggai to rebuild the fallen temple. The Israelite nation struggled during this time to rebuild their city, especially considering that many of the Jews in captivity in Babylon found it more comfortable to stay there than to return to their homeland and help restore it.

To make matters worse, around 168 years before Christ came to this earth, a king named Antiochus Epiphanes IV sought to severely oppress the Jewish nation. A non-canonical historical document called 1 Maccabees states that Antiochus "went up against Israel and Jerusalem with a great multitude, and entered proudly into the sanctuary, taking away the golden altar, the candlestick of light, all the vessels, the table of the showbread, the pouring vessels, the vials, the censers of gold, the veil, the crown, and the golden ornaments before the temple, all of which he pulled off. He also took the silver, gold, precious vessels, and the hidden treasures he found. After taking everything away, he went back to his own land, having caused a great massacre and spoken very proudly. As a result, there was great mourning in Israel, in every place where they were, so that the princes and elders mourned, the virgins and young men became feeble, and the beauty of women changed. Every bridegroom took up lamentation, and she who sat in the marriage chamber was in heaviness. The land also was moved for its inhabitants, and all the house of Jacob was covered with confusion."

This might seem as though the nation would be ended, but they were not left without hope. A man named Judas arose in Israel and fought against their adversaries. As the story goes, when Judas had only a small company of faithful men to fight by his side and was faced with a great multitude of strong warriors, it seemed they had no chance. However, Judas spoke and said, "It is no hard matter for many to be shut up in the hands of a few; and with the God of heaven, it is all one to deliver with a great multitude or a small company. For the victory of battle does not stand in the multitude of a host; but strength comes from heaven. They come against us in much pride and iniquity to destroy us, our

74

wives, and children, and to spoil us. But we fight for our lives and our laws. Wherefore the Lord himself will overthrow them before our face, and as for you, be not afraid of them."

Thus, the Israelites fought for their land and law under the guidance of Judas, bringing us to the end of 2 Maccabees where we read, "from that time forth the Hebrews had the city [that is, Jerusalem, the Holy City] in their power." Even this, though, was only temporary. Josephus records that 63 years before Christ, "[Jerusalem] was taken on the third month, on the day of the fast." The Jews were once again in slavery, this time under Roman rule, which continued until Christ came to earth. During this time, there was a constant hope of one who would proclaim liberty to the captives. Jewish thought looked forward to a Messiah who would deliver them from the oppression of their enemies. Today, we see how our Christ does this in a way completely unexpected by the Jews. Let us then, beginning in Verse 31 of John Chapter 8, see why J. P. Lange proclaims Christ in this passage as "THE LIBERATOR OF ISRAEL, THE ADVERSARY OF SATAN, THE HOPE OF ABRAHAM."[19]

John 8:31-36 reads,

[31] So Jesus said to the Jews who had believed him, "If you abide in my word, you are truly my disciples,

---

[19] *John Peter Lange and Philip Schaff, A Commentary on the Holy Scriptures: John (Bellingham, WA: Logos Bible Software, 2008), 285.*

³² and you will know the truth, and the truth will set you free." ³³ They answered him, "We are offspring of Abraham and have never been enslaved to anyone. How is it that you say, 'You will become free'?"

³⁴ Jesus answered them, "Truly, truly, I say to you, everyone who practices sin is a slave to sin. ³⁵ The slave does not remain in the house forever; the son remains forever. ³⁶ So if the Son sets you free, you will be free indeed.

My goal as we travel through this passage is twofold. I believe Christ's teaching and the response of the Jews show us these things that I am going to address. My duty before you and God is simply, to convey this text with as much power as I can in order that the warning is burdensome and the encouragement is comforting.

Let me explain what I just said: We are presented here with two groups of people: those who abide in Christ's word and those who do not. If your life is not given over to Christ's word, then I pray that this chapter would terrify you. That you would see your bondage to sin and live in discomfort and unrest until Christ would free you.

Now for you who abide in Christ's word, I pray that you would rejoice with me! That your sorrow and gloom would turn into leaping and dancing as we, by God's grace, are allowed to see the freedom that Christ has purchased for us. Furthermore, I hope that we, as sons and daughters of God, would live in the freedom that we have and never try to yoke ourselves or any brothers or sisters to the burden of slavery.

There are three points then that I want to make in this chapter, and in all practicality, I'm going to present this text in reverse. I believe what Christ does here is tell us we must abide in his word and then explain the results of doing so. I'm going to proclaim to all of us the freedom we have in Christ and then give the practical exhortation of abiding in His word.

Freedom from Sin

In Verse 31, Jesus tells the Jews who had believed that abiding in His word brings a truth that sets men free. The Jews had absolutely no concept of what He was talking about. As those in bondage to the Romans, they needed a mighty warrior to make Zion a great nation, not truth. From any worldly perspective, this was a really bad approach to war, and as Lange notes, "Freedom is the very thing [the Jews] were bent upon all along; but a political, theocratic freedom, as pictured by a chiliastic mind."[20] In other words, the Jews wanted freedom, but they had no concept of the freedom they needed from sin.

This confusion regarding Christ's statement about them obtaining freedom led the Jews to say in Verse 33 what A. T. Robertson classifies as "a palpable untruth uttered in the heat of controversy."[21] Their response to Christ's proclamation of freedom is that they do not

---

[20] *John Peter Lange and Philip Schaff, A Commentary on the Holy Scriptures: John (Bellingham, WA: Logos Bible Software, 2008), 287.*
[21] A.T. Robertson, *Word Pictures in the New Testament* (Nashville, TN: Broadman Press, 1933), Jn 8:33.

need it. "We are offspring of Abraham and have never been enslaved to anyone." Their claim to the bloodline of Abraham is true enough, but it helps them nothing with their situation before Christ. Regarding their claim to have never been enslaved, it's lacking at best.

As we already unfolded, the offspring of Abraham were always enslaved; their covenant condemned them time and time again. But even this fails to get at the heart of what Jesus is saying. Christ's reply in Verse 34 speaks of a much deeper slavery under a much crueler master. ESV renders this verse really well: "everyone who practices sin is a slave to sin." The whole dynamic of the conversation has just taken a deep turn. Those who live in Christ's word live in freedom; those who live in disobedience to Christ's word are in slavery, and in Verse 35, the slave is cast out.

That claim to Abraham's lineage that these Jews just made turned around and condemned them. You are the offspring of Abraham. You received the oracles, the law, the prophets. God spoke to you through His servants in many times and in many ways. He provided for you with special care and sent many men to warn you of the dangers of disobedience. When you were a young and helpless people, God took you under His wing and gave you all you could ever need until you grew into a great army able to fight and be established. Yet still, you disobeyed.

The law that was given to you with great glory and fire. A loud voice thundered from the heavens and gave you commandments to walk in and follow - you did not follow it. The great God who bought you and redeemed you from slavery to your enemies, you abandoned Him and sold yourself back into slavery. Not just physical slavery - you worshiped false gods and committed great abominations - you sold yourself into sin. Yes, you are the offspring of Abraham, and all the blessings you were given will rise up against you on the day of judgment to condemn you.

You know that it is wrong to lie, so why is it that you deceive your neighbor? Why are you so willing to cheat in order to win? You know God has said not to dishonor your Father and Mother, so why do you argue with them? How is it that you so eagerly disobey when they are not there to correct you? That sin that you live in, you are enslaved to it - and the slave gets cast out of the house.

But the Jews did not understand this; their appeal to themselves as Abraham's children was an appeal to the promise of Abraham and to his offspring. A promise of a nation that is greater than all the other nations. One that is living in freedom from any other governing or ruling body. "We are children of promise," they said, "how is it that you say we need freedom?" Their response to Christ's invitation to be made free was not someone who wants freedom; this was the response of someone who is insulted that Christ would insinuate that they are in bondage.

This was not just an insult to them; to say they were in slavery was an insult (in their mind) to their entire lineage. If they are in bondage, then they are not as great as they think they are. So, they ask, how is it that you say 'you will become free'? Christ makes an abundantly clear statement. It's not a physical slavery that the unbeliever battles with. This truth has nothing to do with your position in this world; Christ's statement gloriously transcends that. Every person must deal with the fact that, unless they are freed by Christ, they are enslaved to sin. Everyone who practices sin is a slave to sin. The slave does not remain in the house forever; the son remains forever. So, if the Son sets you free, you will be free indeed.

So, if someone is to be set free from the bondage of slavery, what must happen? In Leviticus 25, a Kinsman Redeemer must have sufficient funds to pay back the amount owed by the one who sold himself into slavery. When the debt is paid, the slave is free. Here, in John 8, the slave is obeying his master and following the course of this world, the prince of the power of the air. As He is walking about in his chains, unable to free himself from them because his debt is deep. In fact, so deep is this slave's debt that nothing but death can free him from his bonds. The payment for His freedom is that He be crushed for his iniquities, pierced for his transgressions. A slave of such sin ought to be stricken, smitten by God, and afflicted. The Lord ought to put this slave to grief.

And so, at the perfect time, our great Kinsman Redeemer arrives, and He is crushed for our iniquities, pierced for our transgressions. Stricken, smitten by God, and afflicted. It was the will of the Lord to crush Him, and by His wounds, we are healed. If the Son sets you free, you are free indeed!

It is the truth of Christ that sets free the slave. This truth is profound and simple; Christ released us from sin by dying for sin. The punishment for disobedience to the law is death, and so when Christ died, He took the punishment due unto us for our sin. However, what the Bible proclaims is not only that we are free from the punishment of sin but free from sin itself. When we believed upon Christ, our old self was crucified with Christ. Our slavery, in accordance with the law, was only binding as long as we were alive. When our representative died on our behalf, we died with Him and thus are freed from the law and the burden of sin. Thus Romans 6:5-6 can say, "For while we were living in the flesh, our sinful passions, aroused by the law, were at work in our members to bear fruit for death. But now we are released from the law, having died to that which held us captive, so that we serve in the new way of the Spirit and not in the old way of the written code."

Dear Christian, your sin no longer condemns you. The greatest adversary there is will be unable on judgment day to stand before God and speak of any of your sins. If you were to stand before God right now, and the devil were to stand beside you and speak of all the worst things you have ever done. "This man lied, stole, committed adultery. Did you see the way he treated his parents? This man's hands are red with blood." You, with the biggest history of sin, would be standing there draped in the robe of Christ because He was crushed wearing yours. Christ will look at you on that great day of judgment and say, "Well done, good and faithful, enter into the kingdom."

Therefore, you can live right now in freedom. Sin has no grips on you; you're not in bondage to its passions. You can say with Paul, "I delight in the law of God." "For those who live according to the flesh set their minds on the things of the flesh, but those who live according to the Spirit set their minds on the things of the Spirit. For to set the mind on the flesh is death, but to set the mind on the Spirit is life and peace" (Romans 8:5-6). If you continue, now that you are in Christ, to look toward the law, you will never have peace. That law brings nothing but condemnation; thank God that we are free from it.

The 2LBC Chapter 21 says, "the liberty which Christ has purchased for believers under the gospel consists in" — are you ready for this list? — "Consists in their freedom from the guilt of sin, the condemning wrath of God, the severity and curse of the law, and their being delivered from this present evil world, bondage to Satan, and dominion of sin, from the evil of afflictions, the fear and sting of death, the victory of the grave, and everlasting damnation: as also in their free access to God, and their yielding obedience unto Him, not out of slavish fear, but a child-like love and willing mind."[22]

Do you understand how extensive this freedom is? Your access to God is not dependent upon your obedience to the law. When you sin, He does not reject you. The times when we struggle to obey Christ's

---

[22] D.W. Barger, editor. The Second London Baptist Confession of Faith (Knightstown, IN: Particular Baptist Heritage Books, 2022), 150.

teaching, we do not need to go to God in fear that He will smite us. Rather, we are enabled by Christ to come to Him as a son comes to a loving father - penitent and repentant, yes - but confident that He will accept us despite our disobedience.

The 2LBC also states in Chapter 19: "true believers are not under the law as a covenant of works, to be thereby justified or condemned."[23] Paul explains it this way in Romans 7: If a married woman were to go and live with another man, she would be called an adulterous. But, if her husband were to die and she were to remarry, she would not be an adulterous. She is only bound to her husband as long as he is alive. Likewise, my brothers, you also have died to the law through the body of Christ, so that you may belong to another, to him who has been raised from the dead, in order that we may bear fruit for God.

I do not know that I am even able to belabor this point enough because it is so amazing. This is where your assurance comes from when you struggle with sin. The Holy Spirit reassures you that you are Christ's, not by pointing you to all the laws that you do keep, but by bringing you in humble repentance before God and seeing your complete dependency on Christ. If you think you are a Christian because you obey God, then you are just like the Jews here who claim to be sons of Abraham. The only claim you have to a right standing before God is your Mediator Jesus Christ.

This is a great joy for us because it frees us to be able to obey God. Before, when we were captives to

---

[23] Ibid, 141.

sin, we were unable to ever please God because our every work was sinful due to our disobedience to the law. Now, in Christ, our disobedience to the law does not exist - we are free to offer up sacrifices of praise to God that are untainted.

Let me quote one more reference from the 2LBC regarding this doctrine. Chapter 21 on Christian Liberty states: "They who upon pretense of Christian liberty do practice any sin or cherish any sinful lust, as they do thereby pervert the main design of the grace of the gospel to their own destruction, so they wholly destroy the end of Christian liberty, which is, that being delivered out of the hands of all our enemies, we might serve the Lord without fear, in holiness and righteousness before Him, all the days of our lives."[24]

In other words, our freedom from the law is not a freedom to disobey but a freedom that enables us to obey! Now that Christ has purchased our freedom, we can, as the 2LBC says, "serve the Lord without fear, in holiness and righteousness before Him, all the days of our lives."[25]   We are free from sin and thereby enabled to not sin. Therefore Reader, proclaim with me this profound truth: **if the Son sets you free, you will be free indeed!**

Be reminded of John 8:35: "The slave does not remain in the house forever; the son remains forever." When we were in slavery to the law and sin, there was no security. If our righteousness is based on our obedience, then we are insecure and enslaved to the

---

[24] Ibid, 154.
[25] Ibid, 154.

rules. We are not slaves in this manner; we are sons and daughters, and our struggles do not change that status. "For all who are led by the Spirit of God are sons of God. For you did not receive the spirit of slavery to fall back into fear, but you have received the Spirit of adoption as sons, by whom we cry, "Abba! Father!" The Spirit himself bears witness with our spirit that we are children of God, and if children, then heirs—heirs of God and fellow heirs with Christ, provided we suffer with him in order that we may also be glorified with him" (Romans 8:14-17).

This provides us with an unshakeable foundation of assurance. The son remains forever; we are sons. Remaining forever necessitates that we live forever.

Freedom from Death

The truth of Christ sets us free from the grips of sin and ultimately sets us free from the cords of death. Most agree that Verse 35 refers generally to sons. In other words, Verse 35 is not speaking specifically of Christ but is instead talking about a principle. A slave can be cast out at any point; a son cannot. The familial relation remains despite the son's actions. Verse 36, however, speaks of one specific person - Christ. "If the Son sets you free, you will be free indeed." So, we are presented with one Son who is mightier than us, One who is able to set us free. A Kinsman Redeemer who has the means to redeem all who come to Him by faith. Not only that, we have a Kinsman Redeemer who not only restores us from sin but preserves us. You will be free indeed! The same adverb was used in Luke 24:34 when Christ rose from the dead and it was proclaimed "the Lord has risen indeed." Really, truly, actually, not halfway, not partial. We are eternally and totally free.

This is the truth that we cling to as Christians. Our Savior was in the grave for three days, yes, but He rose again on the third day. He lives forever. Death has no power over you. The grave has no power over you. The Devil has no power over you. Christ is our victorious King, and He has defeated all of those things. We are set free as sons because Christ has secured us with His status as "the Son." So, **if the Son sets you free, you will be free indeed**!

You, who were dead in your trespasses and the uncircumcision of your flesh, God made alive together with him, having forgiven us all our trespasses, by canceling the record of debt that stood against us with its legal demands. This he set aside, nailing it to the cross. He disarmed the rulers and authorities and put them to open shame, by triumphing over them in him. (Col 2:13-15). Our Redeemer died to the things of this world, and He rose again far above them. By His defeat of death, He has freed us from the bonds of any physical elements. What I mean is that if we are serving Christ, it doesn't matter what type of food you eat, what material you wear, what holidays you celebrate or do not celebrate, or how simple you make your life. I can stand up here in a clown costume, with my iPhone, eating a squid and have the exact same standing with God as someone who wears no color, uses no electronics, and only eats kosher food. We are totally free from the elements of this world.

Colossians 2:16-23 puts it like this: let no one pass judgment on you in questions of food and drink, or with regard to a festival or a new moon or a Sabbath. These are a shadow of the things to come, but the substance belongs to Christ. Let no one disqualify you, insisting on asceticism and worship of angels, going on in detail about visions, puffed up without reason by his sensuous mind, and not holding fast to the Head, from whom the whole body, nourished and knit together through its joints and ligaments, grows with a growth that is from God. If with Christ you died to the elemental spirits of the world, why, as if you were still alive in the world, do you submit to regulations— "Do not handle, do not taste, do not touch" (referring to things that all perish as they are used)—according to human precepts and teachings? These have indeed an appearance of wisdom in promoting self-made religion and asceticism and severity to the body, but they are of no value in stopping the indulgence of the flesh.

Our Christ has risen into the heavens and has freed us from death. All of the elements of this world that will pass away when we die cannot affect our worship. Our Lord is much higher than the passing things of this world. Do not let anyone put you in bondage to their own rules and principles; those things are dying; the Son remains forever. So, **if the Son sets you free, you will be free indeed.**

Conclusion:

Christ's claim in Verse 31 is simple: it's not enough that you simply believe some of what I say; you must continue to believe what I am saying. Or, as A.T. Robertson says, "Your future loyalty to my teaching will prove the reality of your present profession."[26] We have seen many people come through the doors of church who later walked away from the truth. Their profession seemed so sincere at one time, but they did not abide in Christ's word, and so their slavery to sin prevailed, and they went back to their previous life of debauchery.

We are told in Verse 30 that many believed in Christ, and it is upon their belief that Christ exhorts that true belief abides. You see, in classic Johannine fashion, this statement is thoroughly monergistic (exclusively the work of God). If you abide in my word, you are truly my disciples. How does one abide in Christ's word? If the Son sets you free, you will be free indeed. It is the same Holy Spirit who raised our Savior from the dead that regenerates the spiritually dead. If the Son sets you free, dear Christian, you will abide in His word. If the Son has not set you free, then come unto Him this very hour; He is a merciful and faithful Kinsman who will not allow His brothers to perish in sin but will redeem them fully and totally.

And when we abide in Christ's word, we know the truth, and the truth sets us free. This is a constant comfort and assurance as Christians. As we abide in

---

[26] A.T. Robertson, *Word Pictures in the New Testament* (Nashville, TN: Broadman Press, 1933), Jn 8:31.

Christ's word, we are constantly reminded of his precious promises that He has made to us. When sin would rear its sharp fangs, then Christ's word speaks with victory: The law of the Spirit of life has set you free in Christ Jesus from the law of sin and death. When those wicked dogs come and try to enslave us to this world, the triumphant sound of the Scriptures proclaims: We are the circumcision, who worship by the Spirit of God and glory in Christ Jesus and put no confidence in the flesh. And if the fear of death would ever come near to one of God's sons, our great Redeemer speaks forth: **I am the resurrection and the life.**

6

Christ Avenges Blood
Isaiah 62:10-63:6

I pray the preceding chapters have been to your benefit and to His glory. This remaining chapter that lays ahead perhaps serves as the heaviest topic - Christ Avenges Blood.

In Numbers 35, we are presented with a Kinsman Redeemer who has a role that, at first glance, seems quite different than what we have been looking at over the past chapters. The *go-el* in old covenant Israel had several duties that we have looked at; he would redeem a poor brother's land, redeem a poor brother from slavery, or even redeem a poor brother's lineage. Here in this concluding chapter we are speaking of a Kinsman Redeemer who redeems a murdered brother's blood. In ancient Israel, it was the duty of a close relative to put to death a murderer of his brother. Before we delve in let me remind you that a kinsman redeemer's role is to "restore or preserve the full community rights of a disadvantaged family member." In this case, justice says the dead brother deserves that the murderer be put to death.

My goal is not to speak on the death penalty; however, my goal is to point you to Christ. My heart's desire that you see with utmost clarity how our Elder Brother protects you by exacting true and right judgment on our adversaries. That great statement "vengeance is the Lord's" ought to give us comfort and release us from our temptations to exact vengeance ourselves. Although this topic is one of immense weight, my prayer is that we would rest in the fact that Christ cares for his church immensely and does not miss a single wrong done to any one of us. His eyes are as a flame of fire; He sees every wicked and evil thought ever leveraged against His bride and as her great protector, He will repay. His love is immense.

Before we jump into our text, I would like to refresh your memory really quick. The first chapter of this book, we went through Leviticus 25 and spoke upon the general equity of a kinsman redeemer, a word which comes from the Hebrew *go-el*. In the historic books of the Bible, this word is used to describe a covenant relative in Israel who fulfills one of the duties of which we read about. However, in Isaiah, this term begins to be used concerning God. In Chapter 43 Verse 1, our God proclaims to a sunk-down and distraught Israel: Your redeemer is the Holy One of Israel. 59:20

proclaims a Redeemer will come to Zion. Thus, when we look at Isaiah 62:10-63:6 and read about the redeemed, let our minds see that promised Redeemer.

Isaiah 62:10-63:6 proclaims,

¹⁰   Go through, go through the gates;
        prepare the way for the people;
build up, build up the highway;
        clear it of stones;
        lift up a signal over the peoples.
¹¹   Behold, the LORD has proclaimed
        to the end of the earth:
Say to the daughter of Zion,
        "Behold, your salvation comes;
behold, his reward is with him,
        and his recompense before him."
¹²   And they shall be called The Holy People,
        The Redeemed of the LORD;
and you shall be called Sought Out,
        A City Not Forsaken.
63 Who is this who comes from Edom,
        in crimsoned garments from Bozrah,
he who is splendid in his apparel,
        marching in the greatness of his strength?
"It is I, speaking in righteousness,
        mighty to save."
² Why is your apparel red,
        and your garments like his who treads in the
            winepress?
³ "I have trodden the winepress alone,

and from the peoples no one was with me;
I trod them in my anger
and trampled them in my wrath;
their lifeblood spattered on my garments,
and stained all my apparel.

Who is being Redeemed? (62:10-12)

Our very first verse, Verse 10 of Chapter 62, gives this command to go through the gates. It seems as though this message is being heralded out so that the hearers will know to clear the road, make sure that the path is ready and smooth. Perhaps some masses of people are coming through these gates, and the roads must be prepared for them. The repetition here is alarming, drawing our attention and preparing us for something great. At the end of this verse, a signal is being raised over the peoples, there's a message going out calling this group into this city. So, we come to these gates with eager anticipation, ready to see what all of the hollering is about. The very next verse tells us what city it is: "The Lord has proclaimed to the end of the earth: 'say to the daughter of Zion.'"

The daughter of Zion is most likely a poetic way of saying Jerusalem, and even more specifically, the inhabitants. Zion was a great hill in Jerusalem, and if you looked down from atop it, you would see that great city with all of her people bustling about. This term, daughter of Zion, is used numerous times by Isaiah throughout his prophecies, but it's not always used in so great a way as we see it used today. In the opening chapter of this book, Verse 8, the prophet proclaims "the daughter of Zion is left like a booth in a vineyard, like a lodge in a cucumber field, like a besieged city." Speaking of the debauchery of Judah, the Lord says in Isaiah 3:16-17 "the daughters of Zion are haughty and walk with outstretched necks, glancing wantonly with their eyes, mincing along as they go, tinkling with their feet, therefore the Lord will strike with a scab the heads of the daughters of Zion, and the LORD will lay bare their secret parts."

Therefore, the message comes to us to enter through the gates, and we are at a loss as to why this is such a great proclamation. Enter through the gates of Jerusalem? The besieged city? The land of ruin, forsaken by God? Oh, but Our Lord is not slack concerning His promises. The daughter of Zion was destroyed, the city was laid waste, the walls broken down, and the temple demolished. If our Lord is not slack concerning His promise of their destruction, we must trust that He is not slack concerning this promise we read of today either! "Say to the daughter of Zion: Your salvation comes!". Those who have been exiled are called to come back to their city, a signal is raised that it is time for them to return. In the words of Calvin: "...there shall be a free passage through the gates of the city, which formerly were shut or in a ruinous state; shut when it was besieged by enemies; in a ruinous state, when the city was thrown down and levelled with the ground. [The Prophet] means that there shall be such a restoration of the city, that its inhabitants shall be numerous, and there shall be frequent passing to and from it."[27]

But that is not all: salvation, reward, and recompense are all spoken of in v11. All of those families who have been exiled from their homeland will receive a reward; those who thought it okay to mess with God's people will receive recompense. Because God's people, those spoken of in v12, are His holy ones, His redeemed, sought out, not forsaken. They may have felt forsaken during their exile, but the Lord has never forsaken those whom He foreknew. He is seeking His people out and bringing them into this Jerusalem whose gates are flown wide open for all of these redeemed to enter. A true and effectual redemption, they are sought out and made holy; they shall be called The Holy People. Not like the old covenant where Israel was told by God in Exodus 19:5-6: if you will indeed obey my voice and keep my covenant, you shall be my treasured possession among all peoples…and you shall be to me a kingdom of priests and a holy nation." We find no "if" here in Isaiah 62; this is a promise from God.

It is promises like this that the Apostle Peter calls to mind when he refers to Christ's church in 1 Peter 2:9 as "a chosen race, a royal priesthood, a holy nation, a people for [God's] own possession." Our passage today is by no means limited to those who received this prophecy when it was given. The call to enter the gates

---

[27] John Calvin and William Pringle, *Commentary on the Book of the Prophet Isaiah*, vol. 4 (Bellingham, WA: Logos Bible Software, 2010), 331.

of this great city is much farther-reaching than that. All of those who are called the Holy People, every single person who is redeemed by the Lord, those whom God seeks out, are a part of this city that is not forsaken. We are holy right now; we have been redeemed by Christ, amen!? But, as Motyer observes, this passage speaks of "the finally perfected people, living in the full reality of a finished salvation." It speaks of the "redeemed: those to whom the Lord made himself Next-of-Kin, taking all their needs as his own." This passage speaks of the full reality of our future Jerusalem, where "Every former woe is a thing of the past.[28]"

It is only right that a signal is raised over the peoples, that we are called to come through the gates and to clear the way for entrance into this city. This city is the fullness of all of God's promises being realized. When the church enters this city, we will have dominion over the earth, all that God spoke to Abraham will be brought to fulfillment - the land of Canaan will be inherited! Remember that promised rest that we spoke of two weeks ago? This is that city.

But who is it that will bring this to pass? We all want to give the Sunday school answer and exclaim "Christ is the redeemer who brings this to pass!" But what if I told you there is much debate over who this is speaking of among respected scholars. The great

---

[28] J. Alec Motyer, Isaiah: An Introduction and Commentary, vol. 20, Tyndale Old Testament Commentaries (Downers Grove, IL: InterVarsity Press, 1999), 433.

expositor John Calvin does not believe that Chapter 63 is speaking of Christ. Many believe this is something that has already been fulfilled in the Maccabean revolt. This brings me to my next point:

Who is the Redeemer? (63:1)

To quote Robert Lowth:

> *"It is by many learned interpreters supposed, that Judas Maccabeus and his victories make the subject of [this prophecy]. What claim Judas can have to so great an honour, will, I think, be very difficult to make out; or how the attributes of the great person introduced can possibly suit him. Could Judas call himself the announcer of righteousness, mighty to save? Could he talk of the day of vengeance being in his heart, and the year of his redeemed being come? or that his own arm wrought salvation for him...though this prophecy must have its accomplishment, there is no necessity of supposing that it has been already accomplished...We need not be at a loss to determine the person who is here introduced as stained with treading the wine-press, if we consider how St. John in the Revelation has applied this image of the Prophet; Rev. 19:13, 15, 16.*[29]

[29] Robert Lowth, Isaiah: A New Translation, with A Preliminary Dissertation and Notes (Boston; Cambridge: William Hilliard; James Munroe and Company, 1834), 388–389.

Lowth is clear: the great attributes of this Redeemer do not fit Judas Maccabeus. I expounded for a little while last chapter about the great accomplishment of Judas in his fight against tyranny and oppression of the Jewish nation. But the man in this prophecy treads the winepress alone. The Redeemer of Isaiah 63 has much greater results than Judas ever had. Let us look, then, at the Redeemer here in Verses 1-2.

The question is asked in Verse 1: Who is this? This Redeemer is coming out of that bloody nation Edom; He is splendid in His apparel and marching in the greatness of His strength. It is only right that the question be asked, who is this? There seems to be, in the distance, this great and marvelous-looking man, whose clothing is honorable and strength magnificent. As the prophet beholds this man marching toward him, he asks: who is this?

The answer comes, making the needy leap with joy: "It is I, speaking in righteousness, mighty to save." Perhaps, as much as we know about the passage so far, "I" could refer to anybody. But if you would, take a step back with me into the context of the passage we have read this morning - turn to Isaiah 61. In Verse 1, someone proclaims: "The Spirit of the Lord GOD is upon me, because the LORD has anointed me to bring good news to the poor; he has sent me to bind up the brokenhearted, to proclaim liberty to the captives, and the opening of the prison to those who are bound; to proclaim the year of the LORD's favor, and the day of vengeance of our God; to comfort all who mourn."

This is the exact verse Jesus quotes in Luke 4:18, and it matches exactly with what the Redeemer in our passage today is doing. Not only that, but as I already quoted from Robert Lowth, Revelation 19:15 uses this very passage to speak of the judgment enacted by Christ at the end of this world as we know it.

How is This Redemption Accomplished (63:1-6)?

Perhaps this Chapter has been a little hard to follow so far, but I pray it will all take shape as we seek to understand this last point.

In Verse 11 of Chapter 62, we are told that when Christ comes as Redeemer, He brings both reward and recompense. As we look at Verses 1-6 of Chapter 63, I want us all to see that the destruction of the wicked is a necessary part of our redemption. One of the greatest promises that we find in Christ and His resurrection is that death and sin will be no more. What we have looked at in Christ in the last weeks is how He frees us from death and sin. We have gloried in the fact that our Kinsman Redeemer took the debt that we owe and was crushed for our sins on the cross in order that we can rise to eternal life following Him.

As I noted at the beginning of this chapter, however, there is another side to the Kinsman Redeemer. He also must exact vengeance on those enemies of His brothers. Christ has defeated sin and death for us by taking our sin and death upon Himself. He defeats the sin and death of His enemies by destroying them. Thus, what I conveyed earlier will come to pass: this great city filled with Holy People - a place where sin and death do not exist. Whether by justification or by annihilation, they have been done away with.

Let us turn our eyes to Isaiah 63:1 and glory in our Redeemer. Edom here is a city founded by Esau; if you remember who Esau is, you may remember that there was a promise made to him by Isaac. Isaac pronounced a prophetic blessing on Esau in Genesis 27:40 that said he would live by his sword and serve his brother. His brother was Jacob, later named Israel. So Edom was in constant submission to Israel for many years. However, the prophecy went on to say that Esau would grow restless and break the yoke of servitude from his neck. Thus, Edom was historically a restless nation and a great enemy of Israel. Delitzsch notes here: "Edom, which dwelt in Israel's immediate neighborhood, and sprang from the same ancestral house, hated Israel with hereditary mortal hatred, although it knew the God of Israel better than Babylon ever did because it knew that Israel had deprived it of its birthright, viz., the chieftainship. If Israel should have such a people as this, and such neighboring nations generally round about it, after it had been delivered from the tyranny of the mistress of the world, its peace would still be incessantly threatened. Not only must Babylon fall, but

Edom also must be trodden down before Israel could be redeemed or be regarded as perfectly redeemed."[30]

Did you follow that? The hatred and enmity that came out of Edom were not like the other world powers that warred against Israel. Edom knew the promises made to Israel; it knew the God of Israel and the power that rightfully belonged to Jacob, yet he rebelled and hated him. Israel's other enemies simply wanted to conquer Israel because they were a nation, and kingdoms like Babylon wanted to be powerful and conquer everybody. Edom, on the other hand, specifically and prophetically, was against Israel.

There's another name that appears here: Bozrah. Bozrah is the capital of Edom, and its name means "inaccessible" or "enclosed." Lexham Bible Dictionary says, "it was protected by steep ravines on three sides." Edom was not an easy kingdom to fight; they were enemies of Israel and wanted the yoke of Jacob broken from their neck. Therefore, if Israel's Kinsman Redeemer is to restore and preserve their full community rights, then those who resist them must be compromised. But not only compromised, they must be done away with entirely. In order for them to inherit the greatness of the blessing made to Abraham, those who oppose God's kingdom must be put to shame.

But, as Lange says, and this will only be substantiated when we look at Revelation 19 later, "Edom is a representative people. It is not an

---

[30] Carl Friedrich Keil and Franz Delitzsch, Commentary on the Old Testament, vol. 7 (Peabody, MA: Hendrickson, 1996), 593.

emblematic name of the great world-power, in its violence and tyranny, for which Babylon is made to stand. But Edom, the inveterate enemy of Israel, and occupying a bad pre-eminence in hatred against Israel, is the representative of the world that hates the people of God."[31] Therefore, if our Kinsman Redeemer is to restore and preserve our full community rights, then those who resist Christ's bride must be compromised. But not only compromised, they must be done away with entirely. In order for us to inherit the greatness of the blessing made to Abraham, those who oppose God's Kingdom must be put to shame.

This Redeemer, who in Verse 1 proclaims Himself as mighty to save, brings salvation in Verses 2-6 by trampling His church's enemies. "It is redemption," says Motyer, "the loving act of the Kinsman, who cannot bear that his next-of-kin should suffer any more or any longer but longs that they should be rescued."[32] "The vengeance," adds Delitzsch, "applies to those who hold the people of God in fetters and oppress them; the grace to all those whom the infliction of punishment has inwardly humbled, though they have been strongly agitated by its long continuance."[33] So it is that this Redeemer comes out of Edom.

---

[31] John Peter Lange et al., A Commentary on the Holy Scriptures: Isaiah (Bellingham, WA: Logos Bible Software, 2008), 671.

[32] J. Alec Motyer, Isaiah: An Introduction and Commentary, vol. 20, Tyndale Old Testament Commentaries (Downers Grove, IL: InterVarsity Press, 1999), 435.

[33] Carl Friedrich Keil and Franz Delitzsch, Commentary on the Old Testament, vol. 7 (Peabody, MA: Hendrickson, 1996), 580–581.

In Verse 2, another question is asked. In Verse 1, the prophet asks who is coming, and the Savior proclaims Himself. In Verse 2, the prophet inquires of Christ, "Why is your apparel red, and your garments like his who treads in the winepress?" And our loving, kind, gentle Savior replies: "I have trodden the winepress alone." This is the work of our Redeemer. Remember, one of the basic requirements for there to be a Kinsman Redeemer is that there be a needy relative. We are not there to help our Christ on the day of this judgment; He treads the winepress alone.

There are those whom the King saves and those whom the King destroys, but our King acts alone. There are needy and helpless sinners who are saved by Christ, and there are prideful sinners who are trampled by Christ, but our Christ here is alone. The picture described is not one of some spirit or invisible power that destroys the enemies of the church. We see here the same Christ who was born in a manger. The child that walked the streets of Jerusalem and was baptized by John in the Jordan. Jesus of Nazareth who taught on the roadside and called children to come sit on his lap. The man who was filled with sorrows and acquainted with grief. Our precious Christ who was crucified in the weakness of human flesh. Who took on Himself our sin, sorrow, and shame.

Our glorious King rose again on the third day, still flesh and bone. The church's Redeemer has gone up to His throne in heaven to sit as a great King above every king and ruler on this earth. He is the one who returns to trample His foes. He needs no help from us in this; we are the redeemed, He is our redeemer.

Delitzsch puts this in such a glorious way when he says,

> "The church that was devoted to Him was itself the object of the redemption, and the great mass of those who were estranged from Him the object of the judgment. Thus, He found Himself alone, neither human cooperation nor the natural course of events helping the accomplishment of His purposes. And consequently, He renounced all human help and broke through the steady course of development by a marvelous act of His own. He trod down nations in His wrath, and intoxicated them in His fury, and caused their life-blood to flow down to the ground."[34]

The Scriptures speak in no uncertain terms about the extent of this destruction for everybody who refuses to submit to Christ's kingdom. Zechariah 14:12 says, "this shall be the plague with which the LORD will strike all the peoples that wage war against Jerusalem: their flesh will rot while they are still standing on their feet, their eyes will rot in their sockets, and their tongues will rot in their mouths." Our Lord will protect His church; He will bring His church to perfection and peace, and to do this, He will pour out vengeance on her adversaries.

---

[34] Carl Friedrich Keil and Franz Delitzsch, Commentary on the Old Testament, vol. 7 (Peabody, MA: Hendrickson, 1996), 595.

Our Savior comes out of Edom, that great enemy of God's people, and pronounces that He has trod the winepress alone. His anger has been poured out, the day of vengeance accomplished. It's on these grounds that we read in Verse 4 that redemption comes. This redemption comes for God's Israel when our Christ marches out of enemy territory proclaiming, "It is I, speaking in righteousness, mighty to save." On that day, The Holy People will dwell secure forever!

As we reach a pinnacle I would like to draw your attention to Revelation 19:11. As I conclude with this passage, you will see very similar statements, some even word for word, with what we just read in Isaiah. But what you will notice is that Edom is not present in name. Rather, we are presented with what I conveyed earlier: People who unite against Christ and His people. Just like in Isaiah 63, these people are trampled.

Conclusion:

Revelation 19:11-21,

[11] Then I saw heaven opened, and behold, a white horse! The one sitting on it is called Faithful and True, and in righteousness he judges and makes war. [12] His eyes are like a flame of fire, and on his head are many diadems, and he has a name written that no one knows but himself. [13] He is clothed in a robe dipped in blood, and the name by which he is called is The Word of God. [14] And the armies of heaven, arrayed in fine linen, white and pure, were following him on white horses.

¹⁵ From his mouth comes a sharp sword with which to strike down the nations, and he will rule them with a rod of iron. He will tread the winepress of the fury of the wrath of God the Almighty. ¹⁶ On his robe and on his thigh he has a name written, King of kings and Lord of lords.

¹⁷ Then I saw an angel standing in the sun, and with a loud voice he called to all the birds that fly directly overhead, "Come, gather for the great supper of God, ¹⁸ to eat the flesh of kings, the flesh of captains, the flesh of mighty men, the flesh of horses and their riders, and the flesh of all men, both free and slave, both small and great." ¹⁹ And I saw the beast and the kings of the earth with their armies gathered to make war against him who was sitting on the horse and against his army. ²⁰ And the beast was captured, and with it the false prophet who in its presence had done the signs by which he deceived those who had received the mark of the beast and those who worshiped its image. These two were thrown alive into the lake of fire that burns with sulfur. ²¹ And the rest were slain by the sword that came from the mouth of him who was sitting on the horse, and all the birds were gorged with their flesh.

So, what does this mean for you and me? We have established that our Kinsman Redeemer, like those *goels* of Old Testament Israel, avenges the blood of our enemies. The Scriptures have shown us the brutal reality of the future of those who rebel against Christ's church. What do we do? We take heart! When the sinfulness and depravity of this world war against us, we call to mind that Christ will destroy them with the brightness of His coming. As the evils of this world all but want to drive us into despair, as worldly men and women make a complete mockery of the Christian faith, we know that our Savior will show the world the glory of His kingdom. We remember that our Savior is our Kinsman and feels and hears every insult, punch, gunshot, and wound that his Church endures - and He will repay.

When we watch as our dear brothers and sisters in other countries are mistreated, our anger boils as we hear of faithful followers of Jesus being martyred by men who hate our God. We look to the heavens where our God has said, "Vengeance is mine, I will repay; In due time their foot shall slip."

In the words of the Apostle Paul:

"This is evidence of the righteous judgment of God, that you may be considered worthy of the kingdom of God, for which you are also suffering— since indeed God considers it just to repay with affliction those who afflict you, and to grant relief to you who are afflicted as well as to us, when the Lord Jesus is revealed from heaven with his mighty angels in flaming fire, inflicting vengeance on those who do not know God and on those who do not obey the gospel of our Lord Jesus. They will suffer the punishment of eternal destruction, away from the presence of the Lord and from the glory of his might, when he comes on that day to be glorified in his saints, and to be marveled at among all who have believed, because our testimony to you was believed." - 2 Thessalonians 1:5-7

Could it be then that presently we get a glimpse of what it will be like when we stand and marvel at our Savior? Or as Christians, when we take communion, look down into that cup filled with the fruit of the vine. Do you see the reason this ordinance is so important to us? There were grapes that were trampled to produce that juice/wine. We have a Christ who was crushed for our iniquity, whose blood flowed from the cross so that we are pardon from that winepress, which will be justly trampled. We rejoice that our Savior has borne the punishment that we so deserved, and we look forward to the day when we will drink the fruit of the vine with Him in His kingdom once He has completely redeemed us from this present evil world.

I find it fitting to cap this book with one final statement from the time-tested 2LBC:

"As Christ would have us to be certainly persuaded that there shall be a day of judgment, both to deter all men from sin and for the greater consolation of the godly in their adversity, so will He have the day unknown to men, that they may shake off all carnal security and be always watchful, because they know not at what hour the Lord will come, and may ever be prepared to say, 'come Lord Jesus, come quickly, Amen.' Come Lord Jesus, come quickly, Amen."[35]

---

[35] D.W. Barger, editor. The Second London Baptist Confession of Faith (Knightstown, IN: Particular Baptist Heritage Books, 2022), 222.

Final Words

Oftentimes, we want to find immediate relevance in each text unto our life today. But may I suggest to you that many times the relevance of the text is not in what you must do but in what Christ has done? Yes, it is true that we can draw many principles from our study of a kinsman redeemer on how we ought to treat our brothers, but all of this is without value if we do not first find Christ to be our Redeemer. Christianity is not a religion of moral superiority, nor is the gospel "love thy neighbor." We preach the good news that one man with a perfect moral status became our brother and redeemed us - this is what all of the shadows in the law looked toward; and Christian: this is more relevant than any other life application I can give you.

I desire that the church would function as the church, and that each of us would be built up loving one another, bearing with one another, admonishing one another, caring for one another as the kinsman doctrine necessitates. Yet, mere pragmatism will never be the answer for achieving such a goal; we must be built up in Christ. The only way one can ever foster a culture of brothers and sisters who love each other is if we are all held by the love of a Kinsman who is efficacious in His work. If the church is going to adhere to the general equity of the law, she must be filled with people who are free from the law and **know** that they are free from the law.

The kinsman redeemer had many functions that, by God's appointment, would keep Israel in momentary peace; may it be proclaimed that our Kinsman Redeemer, by becoming our brother, redeeming us from slavery, renewing the land, and avenging our enemies, brings His church into eternal peace. Would we rest in the arms of our elder Brother, who has secured for us everything needed for our redemption? And knowing this, would we seek to love like our Savior loves us?

This doctrine, the one that is not dependent upon me, is much more glorious than any law could ever be. May we cast away all pragmatic thought and see truly how relevant Christ is to affect our every action! It is the preaching of the law as fulfilled by Christ that pulls my heart to ministry. When I see my Savior as having so sufficiently done what I could never do, then I desire nothing but to love Him and His people. Away with law-centered living; give me Christ, for He alone can truly subdue my flesh to His holiness.

Bibliography

Alexander Souter, A Pocket Lexicon to the Greek New Testament (Oxford: Clarendon Press, 1917).

Alfred Edersheim, Bible History: Old Testament, vol. 2 (Grand Rapids, MI: William B. Eerdmans Publishing Company, 1975).

Andrewes, John. The Golden Cabinet of True Treasure. London: John Crosley, 1615. Early English Books Online Text Creation Partnership, 2011.

A.T. Robertson, *Word Pictures in the New Testament* (Nashville, TN: Broadman Press, 1933).

Brown, Hebrews, 137. Quoted by Martin. Exegetical and Theological Commentary on the Epistle to the Hebrews. Trinity Pulpit Press, Montville, New Jersey, 2020.

Carl Friedrich Keil and Franz Delitzsch, Commentary on the Old Testament, vol. 7 (Peabody, MA: Hendrickson, 1996).

D.W. Barger, editor. The Second London Baptist Confession of Faith (Knightstown, IN: Particular Baptist Heritage Books, 2022).

Ebrard, Hebrews, 349. Quoted by Martin. Exegetical and Theological Commentary on the Epistle to the Hebrews. Trinity Pulpit Press, Montville, New Jersey, 2020.

James Strong, A Concise Dictionary of the Words in the Greek Testament and The Hebrew Bible (Bellingham, WA: Logos Bible Software, 2009), 64.

James Swanson, Dictionary of Biblical Languages with Semantic Domains: Greek (New Testament) (Oak Harbor: Logos Research Systems, Inc., 1997).

J. Alec Motyer, Isaiah: An Introduction and Commentary, vol. 20, Tyndale Old Testament Commentaries (Downers Grove, IL: InterVarsity Press, 1999), 435.

John Calvin, Institutes of the Christian Religion & 2, ed. John T. McNeill, trans. Ford Lewis Battles, vol. 1, The Library of Christian Classics (Louisville, KY: Westminster John Knox Press, 2011).

John Calvin and James Anderson, *Commentary on the Book of Psalms*, vol. 1 (Bellingham, WA: Logos Bible Software, 2010).

John Calvin and William Pringle, *Commentary on the Book of the Prophet Isaiah*, vol. 4 (Bellingham, WA: Logos Bible Software, 2010.

John Owen, An Exposition of the Epistle to the Hebrews, ed. W. H. Goold, vol. 21, Works of John Owen (Edinburgh: Johnstone and Hunter, 1854).

John Peter Lange et al., A Commentary on the Holy Scriptures: Isaiah (Bellingham, WA: Logos Bible Software, 2008).

Matthew Henry, Matthew Henry's Commentary on the Whole Bible: Complete and Unabridged in One Volume (Peabody: Hendrickson, 1994).

M'Lean, Hebrews, 119. Quoted by Martin. Exegetical and Theological Commentary on the Epistle to the Hebrews. Trinity Pulpit Press, Montville, New Jersey, 2020.

Legacy Standard Bible (Three Sixteen Publishing, 2022).

Robert Lowth, Isaiah: A New Translation, with A Preliminary Dissertation and Notes (Boston; Cambridge: William Hilliard; James Munroe and Company.

Robert Martin, Exegetical & Theological Commentary on the Epistle to the Hebrews (Trinity Pulpit Press, 2020).